The Rush to Resurrection

THE RUSH TO RESURRECTION

DONALD X. BURT, O.S.A.

THE LITURGICAL PRESS
COLLEGEVILLE, MINNESOTA

Library of Congress Cataloging in Publication Data

Burt, Donald X.
    The rush to resurrection.

    1. Lent—Prayer-books and devotions—English.
I. Title.
BX2170.L4B83   1985   242'.34   85-23096
ISBN 0-8146-1440-X

Dedication

To Rosalie: In Memory of a Rush to Resurrection
Bravely Run

A Matter of Style

St. Augustine is frequently quoted in this book. Rather than burden
the reader with a series of "Augustine says" phrases, I ask that this
concession be made: a work cited without noting the author should
be assumed to be from the works of St. Augustine.

Contents

The Rush to Resurrection

One certain fact about our lives just now is that they are on the move. Heraclitus, that ancient Greek philosopher, compared human life to a rushing river. St. Augustine said that it was more like a flowing song. Both agreed that we are on the move. But where?

The testimony of my experience is that I am rushing towards death. This thing that I call "me" is in constant process of building up and breaking down. I am constantly coming and going. Eventually more of me will go than will come, and I will die. Nature tells me that my life may be a song, but eventually death will come and that will be the end of *that* tune. It is not absolutely impossible that I may survive death, but there are no good scientific reasons supporting that contention. I am so imbedded in my physical existence that it is hard to even imagine what such a life after death might be like. I have had no personal experience of such life. Oh, I do make great claims for the dignity of my spiritual activity in my great thoughts, my great dreams, my great plans, but just as I am ready to soar beyond my here and now, my head begins to ache or I get hungry or I am overpowered by other physical needs and am dragged back to that crusty earthen thing that is me. If I try to understand my life simply on the basis of my own experience, it is hard to escape the conclusion that I am rushing to my death and nothing more.

However, there is another way of knowing that goes beyond concrete experience. It is the way of faith. By faith I come to believe facts about my life because of the testimony of someone I trust. It is not an unreasonable way to know, even though there are no coercive reasons forcing me to believe. Faith like love is a decision. It presents an invitation to trust, and once trust is given it provides the strength to act on the decision made. Through faith I can come to know something more about my life. I am no longer tied down by the limited information provided by experience. The person of faith is something like the baby eagle pushed from its nest by its doting mother. Only by taking an unreasonable leap can it experience the thrill of flight. Reason says that to jump from the ledge is to die. The only safe course is to sit in the nest and hope for the best. But to do so is to be imprisoned in a jail created by the mind. It is trapped in place by its fear of the unknown, by its reluctance to act without good reasons. I am like the eagle in my fears and in my challenge. If I do not leap beyond my experience, I shall die for lack of nourishment. My needs are simply too broad to be satisfied on this arid ledge of good reasons.

But it is not easy to let go. Even St. Augustine clung to such a ledge for many years. He tried to understand his life through any and all rational approaches offered by his world. But finally he took his leap into the darkness and learned that he had to believe before he could understand the important things of life. In order to understand what his life was about, where he was rushing, he first had to believe in someone who knew the answer. That one was Jesus. St. Augustine tried everything he knew and then took his leap into the unknown. He flew with Jesus to the heights of time and peeked into eternity. He looked down from his lofty perch on the arm of God and saw his earthly life as it truly was. He saw that he was rushing to death and more: he was rushing through death to resurrection. And so am I. And so are you.

This is the theme of the pages that follow. I am rushing to resurrection. It is the message that comes from my belief in Jesus. Perched on his arm, I can see my whole life for the first time. I can see beyond that narrow fragment that is my time just now. From the perspective of Jesus, I can see my resurrection as a fact, just as my rushing is a fact and my death is a fact. Indeed, Jesus exemplified my life in his own human life. He too rushed towards resurrection. Long ago he showed me what a rush towards resurrection might be like. And then he called me into existence so that I could start my own rush. Why me? Because for some strange reason he wanted *me* as his companion in life. By my conception I was inserted into the life, death, and resurrection of the Incarnate Son of God. His history is also my history. By watching him I can learn how to live.

Each year I am invited to relive the days of Jesus with him. Especially in Lent I am reminded of the days when he was making his rush to resurrection. Those forty days stand for the earthly life of every human. We are all making our own rush in our own special way, but we have much in common with each other and with Jesus. Thus he invites us again and again in our earthly life to relive his last forty days. He invites us to run with him on his rush through death. By so doing, we can practice for our own and perhaps not be so afraid.

This is the purpose of the pages that follow: to remind myself of Jesus' last forty days and to learn from them something important about my life and about my death. My life is brief; my death is certain. But I should not be afraid. I am rushing towards resurrection, and my God is holding my hand.

Mardi Gras: Wombed Waiting

The first great mystery of my life is that before my beginning I had already received a call to be. Out of all the infinite possibilities open to him, God chose *me* to be. He *wanted* me. He loved me into existence with a love more powerful than the love that joined my parents in their conceptive act. My parents gave me something of themselves, but God gave me everything. He called me from nothingness. He created this special Donald, this unique (if not odd) person, D.X.B., who had never existed before. Once having made me, he continued to support me. He puffed life into me fifty odd years ago and now holds firm within my fragile walls that precious air. I had my first Christmas before my time began. Before I came to be, the Lord came to me. He came to make me. Only then did I begin my rush to resurrection.

In the beginning there was the womb. That was the place where my rush began. It was an unconscious process at first. I did not know what was happening, where I was, or where I was going. I was aware of some things, however (though not conscious of my awareness). My mother said that she felt me moving. I was already stretching toward goals as yet unperceived. I was already hungry to be out and about. My mother was the first witness to the new traveler towards eternity. She was the first human to perceive that new spark of life that was never to be extinguished. Like every human mother she nourished eternity in her womb. As for me, I was too busy eating and sleeping to be concerned. It was my time of Mardi Gras, the last time for me to ignore my future without penalty, the last time when I could ignore my past because I had no past to remember. In the womb if I had had a mind to, I could have taken as my motto, "Let me eat and drink today, for tomorrow I must die."

In those early moments of my existence, I was already experiencing great truths about human living. Even in my first days I depended on the strength and suffering of another. As I was being carried by the gracious love of my mother, I was being taught how I must live my days on earth: supported by the love of humans, divine grace, and the cross of the Incarnate Lord. I was on my way in the arms of one who loved me, and no one knew where my path would lead, no one, that is, except the Lord who led me. I imagine that even then he was praying for me as he prays for all the unborn: "I pray, Father, that where I am they also someday shall be."

My first days in the womb were like pre-Lenten days here in the North. It was very dark. I was moving towards light, but I did not know it as I slept quietly in the hug of my mother's womb. I was being nourished but did not realize it. I was moving but not yet purposefully. I was already reacting to my environment. And, most wonderful of all, I was already fixed in the gaze of that Infinite One who had said "Yes" to my existence.

It was the beginning of my rush from dark to light, from nothing to everything. I waited in the womb for the day when I had to take responsibility for my destiny.

Ash Wednesday: Celebration

Ash Wednesday symbolizes the beginning of my conscious rush to resurrection. I exist, and I know now something about what my life entails. I know that I am moving down the road towards my own personal easter. I know that I must pass death to get there. How should I feel about my prospects? Jesus tells me not to be glum (Matt 6:16). To believe is a cause of joy.

It is certain that someday I shall die, and that fact is not exhilarating. Fear is natural facing death. Indeed, St. Augustine said that if someone claims to be unafraid of death, he may already be dead (*Sermon 348*). But even death is less fearful if we can come to see it as the Lord describes it, a going home with him. We have never experienced life after death, but others have told us that it involves great happiness. St. Augustine says simply that "We shall be drunk with the richness of God's house" (*Commentary on Psalm 35, #14*). We shall be overcome with joy because we shall see God face-to-face. Now we can "more easily say what God is not than what he is" (*Commentary on Psalm 85, #12*). But even now, through faith, we can know that if we are true to God in this life, we *shall* someday go home with him. We can know that someday *we shall see God.* How do we know? Through the promise of Jesus. Jesus has said to us: "This is eternal life: to know the one true God" (see John 17:3). And when that great day comes for us, we shall be very happy because we shall be "glued to God by love" (*Commentary on Psalm 62*, #17).

But that is my future; my present is not always that pleasant. Just now I am part of that human race that is still like a sick giant (*Sermon 87:11*). I live in a world that is passing away, a world that is "short of breath" (*Sermon 81:8*). May I not be rightfully sad about my present condition? Ashes seem a proper symbol of my life just now, a life that feels like it is fading away. But I must not judge my life with the measure of my feelings. I must get outside of myself to get the true picture. Even in a Lenten time the "world smiles with many brilliant and beautiful things" (*Sermon 158:7*). Inside I may feel gray and ashy, more dead than alive. But my world, the world in which I live and work out my future, is bright and blue and full of promise. I live in a world in which I shall forever be more alive than dead.

I remember one year in New England when Lent blew in on the wings of a memorable winter storm. Ash Wednesday dawned all blue and white and crisp. The world was covered by pure snow as I entered the chapel for my dab of ash. I could not feel ashy on such a day. The brilliance of the day reinforced my hope that I might be immortal after all. The ash reminded me that death was a part of my life, but the snow reminded me that life is forever. Indeed, it seemed to be a better symbol of my future. It was truer to what my life would be. I thought to myself: "Perhaps we should put snow on our brows as we begin our Lent. Ashes are not nourishing. Snow can slake one's thirst. Snow is refreshing. Even a small amount cools the skin. And it reminds of resurrection rather than death. It is like the glorified body of that humble water that is so necessary for life just now. Perhaps a bit of snow is a better symbol of my rush to resurrection."

As my Lenten journey begins, I am reminded that I am in the process of dying, but I must never forget that my dying is part of my process of living forever. I must be joyful as I begin because I am going to meet the Lord. I must be joyful on the way because even now I am not alone. As St. Augustine proclaimed to his people: "Wherever you are on earth, however long you remain on earth,

'The Lord is near!' Do not be anxious about anything" (*Sermon 171:1-5*).

Thursday after Ash Wednesday: Things

When we get to heaven, we shall no longer need things. We shall only love people. We shall finally be able to forget about "earning a living" and just *live.* It is quite different now. We seem to need more and more things just to get through our daily life, and we seem to need more and more time to earn the things we need. There is nothing wrong in having some things. Being poor is no guarantee of virtue. As St. Augustine said, "What advantage is there to stand with empty hands if your heart is filled with the desire for everything?" (*Commentary on Psalm 51:14*). Whether we have things or do not have things, we must be free to love the Lord. Just now we need some things in order to survive, but we must not come to depend on them too much. We must not be captured by them.

We want to live secure lives, and there is nothing wrong with that. But to be secure on this earth, we must have food and drink and shelter. We truly need these good things, and one of the modest joys of this life is in fulfilling these natural needs in fine fashion. We seek not any old place to live. The dream of every human is to have a "nice" place. We rejoice in a good meal and pure refreshing drink. But sometimes our passion can get the better of us. Even when we have the good things of life, we are still unsettled. We worry about keeping them. We worry about the day when we may lose them. We begin to act like autumn squirrels, gathering nuts for a winter we may never live to see. We say to ourselves: "Who will take care of me when I am old and gray? Perhaps if I gather more and more things now, then I will be able to buy the care I need on the day when there is no one to care for me." We gather more and more to secure our life and worry more and more that it is not enough. We are very sad in the midst of all our things.

We also want our lives to have some importance, and there is nothing wrong in that. We want to be a success, and sometimes we become convinced that our success is measured by the things we have. If others will not "look up to us" as persons, we hope that they will look up to us in our things. We hope that others will look at our house and say, "It must be a fine person who lives in such a fine place." Our money buys the attention that we fear we do not deserve. Our radio makes talk just for us. Our television makes entertainment just for us. We can turn off our things and through them the people who perform for us. We have power over people and this makes us feel important. But when all our things are quiet, we discover that we are alone. We are very sad in the midst of all our things.

We want to be loved, and there is nothing wrong with that. But we are sometimes silly in our attempts to attract love. We hope that fine clothes will do the trick—or a nice car or the promise of exotic trips. We give expensive presents in order to be remembered with affection. We give our things instead of ourselves, because to give oneself to a love is to become vulnerable. We fear being rejected by the loved one. We fear that we may be the wrong size for them or the wrong style. And thus we give them our things rather than our love, saying: "It is less painful to exchange a rejected gift than a rejected heart." Or we may just not want to be bothered by our loves. We are willing to be loved, but we do not wish to be bound down. Thus we try to hold our loves by giving them watches rather than our time. We gather around us all these good things for buying love and find that they do not work. We are very sad in the midst of our things.

We want things in order to be free, and there is nothing wrong with that. But we make a mistake in believing that things will buy freedom. Our things may free us from dependence on others, but in the process we find a new prison. We become entrapped by our things. We have gained everything and lost ourselves. Perhaps then we remember the warning of the Lord: "What profit does he show who gains the whole world and destroys himself in the process?" (Luke 9:25). We remember, and in the midst of our things we are very sad.

We must be careful that we are not destroyed by our things in this world. There is nothing wrong with having them. They are part of God's creation and are good. But they are also things of the here and now. They are stuck in place while we are on the move. If we clutch them too tightly, we can be held back from our future. They cannot come with us. We shall run through death towards resurrection with nothing but our memories. We are well advised not to be encumbered by a lot of useless baggage. We are well advised not to enlarge our estate so that we might be comfortable at the end. Tolstoy's answer to the question, "How much land does a person need at the very end?" is true for all of us: "About six feet . . . just enough for a grave."

Friday after Ash Wednesday: Playing on the Road

Jesus was not opposed to having a good laugh once in a while (and perhaps that is why he called me and you into existence). He liked to play with children. He went to banquets. He seemed to like weddings. Indeed, he was quite vehement against those who criticized the first Christians for being happy. He said: "How can wedding guests go in mourning so long as the groom is with them? When the day comes that the groom is taken away, then they will fast." (Matt 9:1). What I hear him saying is that in my life there will be good days and bad days, and it is no sin to be a little goofy somedays.

We humans are going to die. We humans are even now rushing towards our resurrection. But these important truths should not stop us from having some fun on the way. Just because we are grown up and winding down is no reason for giving up times of play. I am an old fossil now. I no longer run in short pants. I breathe in short pants. But I still need some time to play. I am a social fossil; thus I can always use someone to play with me. Jesus tells me that there is nothing wrong with that. God lives! I am alive! The Bridegroom is here! What better reason for a human to rejoice?

When we were kids, we did not seem to justify our playing. There was no need. We enjoyed our good times without guilt. A little friend of mine will still turn a somersault at the slightest provocation. She dances in the living room with or without music. She loves to dig in the sand. She sees nothing wrong with an occasional tickle between friends. I hope she never loses her playfulness. Many of us do as we grow older. We lose the gift of being silly for the sake of our spirits. How sad it is to see a human who can only have "fun" when they are high on alcohol or drugs. How sad it is to be able to dance only when unconscious.

Such induced silliness is really no fun at all. Creative silliness demands full attention. Fooling around joyfully cannot be done by fools. To be divinely witless demands that we have our wits about us. The paradox of growing older is that play ceases to be socially acceptable at the precise moment when we become most capable of it. Big folks find it hard to find times for good healthy play. I remember that when I was a kid I could go the playground and easily find a new friend among the strangers. If I were to approach a stranger now with the plea "Come play with me!" the likely result would be incarceration, not recreation. Now that I am big and old, people think me nuts to act nutty. And the kids are the least understanding of our adult whimsies. An adult who is suspected of having a good time is labeled weird. Mothers who dance at teen parties risk being put out for adoption.

It is truly a shame that we find it hard to play as we rush through life. There is no doubt that someday we shall die, but that should not prevent us from doing some fun things in the meantime, such as

taking a roll in the grass,
or lying in a field watching clouds,
or talking quietly to a friend about silly things,
or listening to a loved one laugh.

All of these are fine things to do as we rush towards resurrection, and the Lord favors them.

From the very beginning of his life, Jesus knew that he had to die. He knew that his death would come in his youth and with terrible suffering. But even this terrifying knowledge did not stop him from having fun. He played when he was a child, and when he was a man he held children in his arms. He had devoted men and women who were his friends. He laughed with the impetuous Peter. He talked quietly with Mary. He went fishing with James and John. He worried when Martha seemed to be working too hard and invited her to come and sit with him for a while. He enjoyed wandering in the country. He took trips to the mountains. He dozed in boats drifting on inland seas.

The life and words of the Lord tell us that it is not wrong to play as we make our way towards resurrection. It is not evil to sometimes run with our human loves through the pleasant meadows of this life. It is not a waste of time to sometimes just go out and fly a kite. The bridegroom is still with us, and like him we should have "delight in the sons of men" (Prov 8:31).

Saturday after Ash Wednesday: Illness

Jesus says that the reason he came was to cure the sick (Luke 5:27-32). I say: "Thank God for that!" It is a fine thing to have someone who knows when we are sick and who cares about that unhappy fact. Sickness is a fact of life this side of death. We may complain about it and we may say that it is unfair, but this does not cure us. Indeed, the complaint does not make much sense. We are part of a limited universe which by its very nature tends to fall apart. We are part of a human race which freely chooses to injure itself. We have literally inherited the sins of our ancestors and added to them by our own personal perversity. It is no wonder that St. Augustine speaks of the human species as being a sick giant. We all have our days for feeling rotten.

The worst thing about such days is that we sometimes get little sympathy from others. Some try to understand, but they frequently miss the mark. They say: "So you are sick! How sad! I know *just* how you feel." And then they go on to describe their *own* illnesses. Simone Weil, that powerful philosopher of the human condition, remarked that the special burden of human affliction (which is pain compounded by hopelessness) is that it *cannot* be shared with anyone else. My affliction is peculiarly mine, because it is the straining of my eternal spirit against my weakening body. My spirit fights to be free of that body that is fast falling apart.

It is no one's fault that we are often alone in our illness. Others may truly love us and be worried about our sickness, but they are unable to cope with it. Some are better able to understand their own pain than the pain of those they love. Sometimes our loved ones are just unable to take up their cross of being with us as we bear our cross of illness. They are paralyzed by their own weakness and are unable to show us how much they care. There is a great hurt that comes from such apparent indifference, and it is a hurt that affects the one unable to help more than the one who needs help. Jesus recovered quickly from the pain of Peter's denial, but Peter wept copiously for the rest of his life, because he had been unable to stand by a loved one in a time of need.

It can be some consolation for the sick to know that the indifference of others is not their fault. It is just a fact of life, as much as illness is a fact of life. Jesus-God himself experienced such innocent callousness frequently. For example, it was just after his third prediction of his death that James and John came to him asking for a promotion (Mark 10:32-40). What bad timing! It is a classic example of the "Pass the salt" syndrome, a syndrome found in such dialogues:

"I feel rotten today."   . . . "Oh, is that so? Pass the salt!"
"I am dying today."   . . . "You don't say! Pass the salt!"
"Today your friend died."   . . . "Pass the salt, please."

Jesus did not seem to be upset by human indifference to his suffering. He was not upset when James and John brought their mother along to plead their case. Mothers worried about the future of their sons do not have much energy left to worry about the prospects of their acquaintances. Jesus was not upset when his friends fell asleep in his time of need. The disciples fell asleep in Gethsemane not out of boredom or indifference; they just ran out of steam. Perhaps they had eaten too much at the Last Supper; perhaps they were exhausted by worry over the strange events and perils of their days. In his pain Jesus did not get mad. He knew his friends were only human and that sometimes their best was none too good.

I must try to have such understanding in my own illnesses. Sometimes it is hard. I remember once when I was in the hospital, the staff forgot to bring me breakfast. I felt hurt, abused, and ignored. I assumed the mantle of the great martyr (even though at my size I could have done without a year's breakfasts and been none the worse). In the midst of my sorrow at the cruelty of the staff's indifference, I remembered that my favorite nurse had just lost her husband to alcoholism. I remembered that my favorite nurse-assistant was that day scheduled for tests for suspected cancer. I became ashamed of my displeasure over a missed breakfast. We humans are all in this same hospital together, and sometimes our personal burdens prevent us from attending to the illnesses of others.

Indeed, Simone Weil says there is only one person who truly understands how we feel when we are sick, and that is Jesus-God. That is the God who became a human being to prove his understanding of our illnesses and to cure us of our wounds. That is a fine fact to know; I feel better already.

First Sunday: The Desert in the Garden

When Jesus was in the prime of his life, he suddenly disappeared into a desert. He did not need to go far. God created a garden for his human children, but the desert is never very far from any life this side of death.

This fact of life need not be distressing. A desert is not a place of death. It has its own beauty and vitality. Indeed, John the Baptist seemed to enjoy his desert. Rumor has it that he danced in his wasteland. Certainly a desert is a fine place to pray. Like Jesus we can sometimes hear our Father better in the desert. When we are separated from our earthly delights, we cannot look to them for distraction. In my desert place there is only God and me.

But attitude is important. My desert can be terrifying if I do not accept it in the right spirit. I must be patient. God is not easy to see if I have gotten out of the habit of looking for him. And if I cannot find God right away, I am left only with myself. The sight may be too much to bear. In the starkness of my desert, there are no cosmetics to hide me from myself. In my desert the harsh light may reveal a me that is painful to see.

It is then that the temptations may come, the fantasies that I create to cover the truth of my life:

> the fantasy that I could rule the world if only I can discover a pinnacle high enough;
>
> the fantasy that I can indulge my sensual needs without paying the price for my excesses;
>
> the fantasy that I live in some sort of sanctuary where my foolish acts never do harm to myself or others.

These are the dreams that haunt my desert and make it a place of danger. These are the dreams that separate me from the reality of my life, the reality that cries: "You must search for God and face up to yourself and not depend on any earthly thing for salvation!" My desert proclaims its great worth in loud silence: "There is only the Lord and you. And so it shall be forever."

Once convinced of that truth, I can get on with living a happy life. I can look about and see that even deserts are pretty places. My deserts are part of that wonderful garden the Lord created for me. I can rejoice in being alive and on the way to my resurrection. I can join with St. Augustine in his great hymn to the goodness of this life:

> The great good God has made us humans the loveliest ornaments of this earth. Oh, it is true that we must someday die, but in the

meantime we live in the midst of wonderful things that seem perfectly suited to us. It is true that we have our miseries and that we are sometimes worn out by living, but think of the wonders of this place where we live! Think of the thousands of beautiful things for seeing and thousands of objects just right for making things. There is an infinitely changing beauty in the sky and the land and the sea. What variety of color do we see in the changing moon and sun and stars! There are the soft shadows of noon forests, the shades and smells of spring flowers, the multitudinous melodies and exuberant dress of the birds. There are amazing animals to wonder at . . . the tiny ant even more amazing than the very largest whale. Think of the grand spectacle of the sea vesting itself in its different colors . . . sometimes green, sometimes purple, sometimes the bluest of blue. And how grand it is when there is a storm (especially grand when you are not caught on its heaving surface but are safe on shore and are only caressed by soft mist).

Think of the many foods available to satisfy our hunger! How many tastes there are to tempt even the "picky" appetite! Just think of the many fine things we have that help us stay healthy and the many fine things available to cure us when we inevitably get sick. How grateful should we be for the quiet breeze that kisses us on steamy nights, for the gentle animals and quiet plants that give of themselves so that we might have wool and cotton for our clothes.

This life will not last forever but even so it is possible to have some peace as we go through it. It is possible even now to live in modest good health and without anxiety. It is possible even now to live our lives midst those who care for us. And even though we are destined to lose our earthly loves for a time, there is still hope that someday we shall see them again. And in the meantime we are surrounded by wonders perfectly fitted to us: the light of a good day, the sound of music, air that is just right for breathing, sparkling water that is just fine for drinking. We have everything here that we need to feed our poor old bodies. And we have enough good things left over to help make them pretty (*City of God* 21:13; 22:24).

When my days for dwelling in the desert come (as they must come for every human), I hope that I remember that my desert is in the midst of the garden of the Lord. My world is good even now.

And I am rushing to a world that is even better, a world withou deserts.

Monday of the First Week: A Group Run

As a sometime jogger I envy those folks who do their running in groups. I am amazed that they are able to run and talk at the same time. All my wind is dedicated to staying upright as I ploc along. Those who run in packs can also try great distances. If I coulc run with others, I might be tempted to try new and foreign lands (like the next block) and more difficult terrains. As it is, my solitary running is restricted to soft short tracks so that I may always be only a short crawl from home.

Unfortunately the same system does not work for my run to resurrection. I cannot run my life in circles (though sometimes seem to try). My life's run is a straight course to infinity. There is no safe haven within easy crawl if I should happen to fall on my face. If I am to be saved, I must be picked up by a friend.

Thus in my rush to resurrection, I must not run alone. The race to eternity must be a group run. I cannot run selfishly, indifferen to the needs of others. I cannot run proudly, as though I did no need the help of anyone. I must lean on others, or I shall surely fall. None of us can run alone for very long, but together we can make it through to the end. Together we form one giant persor whose sum seems greater than its parts. We are like a talented relay team which runs as one being and achieves speeds impossible to any one of the members running alone. This is so because wher we run together in love towards our destiny, Jesus the Lord become: one with us. The body that we form has God as its head. In loving each other, we bring Christ to our run. Through our love for eacl other, we insure that Christ runs with us and is there to pick us up and carry us when we fall. As St. Augustine remarked, Jesus our Samaritan carries us to our place of rest on his back (*Sermor 119*, #7).

One of the paradoxes of life is that the infinity of heaven ha: room for only one person, that Mystical Body that has Christ as its head and those who love as its members. There are no isolated individuals in heaven; they are all in hell. Indeed, the special pain of hell is isolation, being forever separated from the Lord.

If our life is a group run, we can be certain that we shall not end up in that terrible solitude. We shall be saved finally and forever if now we care for each other. We shall not fail eternally if now we take seriously the warning of Leviticus: "You shall not . . . stand idly when your neighbor's life is at stake . . . You shall not bear hatred for your brother in your heart . . . You shall love your neighbor as yourself" (Lev 19:16-18). If we take care of each other on the road, we do a divine action, because we take care of the Christ who is present in every human being.

In making our run to resurrection a group run with friends, we insure that Christ is with us even now, and we guarantee that we shall not be left alone when our race is over. We shall cross the end line of this life hand in hand with our friends and our Lord. And we shall realize that so it shall ever be. We shall never be alone for all eternity. Having run this life with love, we shall rise to find ourselves in the house of the Lord.

Tuesday of the First Week: Silent Prayer

One day Jesus told his disciples: "In your prayer do not rattle on like the pagans. They think they will win a hearing by the sheer multiplication of words. Do not imitate them. Your Father knows what you need before you ask him" (Matt 6:7-8).

His words seem a bit testy. He seems to be saying: "Why don't you shut up and say something!" Perhaps he had just finished a staff meeting with the College of Apostles. Academic meetings can sometimes suffocate with words. I know that I often develop a headache from sitting too long at such meetings (an anomaly I will leave to a charitable physiologist to explain). Listening to unimportant points being pounded to death leads to aggravation. Perhaps

Jesus' rule for prayer was a plea, "Don't bore God!" The rule for good prayer is the same as the rule for good committee meetings: "The less said, the better."

It is a comforting message for those of us who cannot seem to come up with any fine prayers. Sometimes I wish there were a divine "Dial-A-Prayer" run by the Holy Spirit with guaranteed results. I wish that there were an agency I could go to, to rent a prayer for the weekend. But it probably would not work for me. I cannot identify with some of those classical prayers in the old prayer books. I get so involved in getting the "Thy's" and "Thine's" straight that I forget about the Lord God that I am supposed to be addressing.

My inability to make a good prayer is especially frightening as I look down the road towards my death. As death comes closer, I may be unable to pray at all. I may become desolated by my inability to talk to God at such a crucial moment. I may feel that I have been left alone by God. I may not feel *him* at all. I may only be able to feel *bad.* The guilt for my lack of religious feeling may increase my fright, as though it were my fault that I am more concerned about Donald's dying than I am about the living Lord.

Jesus tells me not to worry about my silence. The silence of the dying is more precious in God's eyes than all of the needless quacking of the living. When I am dying there is at least a chance that my life will be better focused on the important things, like my rush to resurrection. I do not need to make a lot of noise for God to know what I need and want. God can hear me even better than I can hear myself. St. Augustine tells me that my very desire is a prayer and that prayer stops only when I consciously and coldly turn my back on his love (*Commentary on Psalm 37*, 14).

To need to pray is to pray. To need God is to pray to God. To need a cure is to pray. To need peace is a prayer. To need happiness is a prayer. God knows my needs and will answer those needs (not my *wants* necessarily, but my *needs*). I may not be able to string together any fine words but that makes no difference. God hears my anguish and responds as long as I do not reject him.

Who knows? Perhaps I pray most sensibly through my silence. If I were good with words, I would probably ask for the wrong thing anyway. Fine words tie me to this life and tempt me to ask for something impossible (like never dying) or something improbable (like being cured of a killing disease). St. Augustine warned his people against distracting God by always asking for miracles (*Commentary On Psalm 130*, 13). When he came to the end of his own life, he followed that advice. He did not ask for an improbability: that a weak, sick, seventy-year-old man be restored to health-filled youth. He asked only for a quiet time to pray his prayer of silence. It was granted to him, and in the midst of his prayer God came and cured him by allowing him to rush through death towards resurrection.

Wednesday of the First Week: The Wail of Jonah

The trouble with God is that he knows me too well and is always trying to "fix" me (and St. Augustine says to me, "Well, what do you expect? He *made* you!"). Sometimes he shows me what I am by making me sick. I cannot eat like a horse without being sick like a human. Sometimes he shows me what I am by making me lonely. I cannot act like a jackass without having others run from me. Sometimes he shows me what I am by telling me stories, like the tale of Jonah.

I can identify with Jonah. There he was, making his way peacefully to resurrection, when one day he heard the commanding voice: "Up!" Since there was no elevator in the vicinity, Jonah realized that the voice was that of Jahweh calling him to do a task. It was then that Jonah took up running for his health, taking off as fast as he could due west. He booked passage on a steamer and once on board hid in his bunk. He seemed convinced that God lived only in the old neighborhood and would never think of wandering far from home. Thus, to escape God was easy. All you had to do was take a trip. Jonah was convinced that God was just hanging around Jonah's house waiting to serve Jonah in any way he could. God was Jonah's servant (Jonah thought), and when he became unpleasant, Jonah simply packed up and took a little vacation. Of course it did not work. God is wherever we are and in all places that we are not. Moreover, Jonah could not escape the troubles of life by running away because the trouble with Jonah was Jonah, and *that* baggage he had to take with him everywhere.

Thus his plan for escape was ill-conceived and did not work. God ran with him as he ran away. He boarded the ship with him, hid in the bunk with him, and waved with him to the folks on the dock as the ship pulled out. Then he got down to business. He created a storm and suggested to the frightened sailors that Jonah was to blame. They asked him to go for a swim and accelerated his decision by throwing him overboard. God sent a fish to pick him up, and soon Jonah found himself back on shore after a whale of a ride.

As soon as he recovered from his adventure, the voice came again: "Up!" This time Jonah snapped to attention and followed orders. At God's command he went off to Nineveh and proclaimed God's message: "Straighten out your lives, or in three days you will be destroyed." Much to Jonah's surprise the people believed him and began praying to God for mercy. Jonah relished their fear but would give no relief. He said: "I am the mouth of God, and I say you can all go to hell!" But God intervened and said: "Now wait a minute! They *do* seem sorry, and I am of a mind to forget the whole thing." Jonah replied: "*Well*! You can do anything you like, but I will have no part in it!" And he went off to a hill outside town to sulk. He thought to himself: "How dare God forgive these sinners! Here I have spent all my energy telling them how rotten they are and what God was going to do to them, and now he is going to forgive them. I have wasted my time. I might just as well have stayed home."

Jonah had gone from the belly of a whale to a bellicose wail. Jonah, that new religious paragon, had been suddenly born again. After fleeing from God, he had come to believe that he was God. He cried for retributive justice from a God who had so recently shown him undeserved mercy. The whale was able to keep him down for three days when he was a sinner. Now that he was a self-proclaimed saint, only God could stomach him. Like so many of us, Jonah was more agreeable as a sinner than as a saint.

In any case, God paid no attention to his wailing. He said: "Look, why should I destroy 120,000 people who can't tell their right hand from their left? And besides, why should I kill all the poor animals?" (see Jonah 4:11).

Perhaps God said the same thing to Jonah when his rush to resurrection was over. Perhaps he will say the same thing to me and to you: "Why should I destroy someone who mostly doesn't know their right hand from their left?" It is a consoling thought.

Thursday of the First Week: Esther's Prayer

The Old Testament story of Esther demonstrates that there is no protection from the trials of this life. Even being a queen is no help. The Jewish Esther had everything material she could possibly want from the pagan Xerxes. He was constantly offering her half his kingdom for the pleasure she gave him. There was, however, the nagging insecurity prompted by the rise and fall of his previous queen, Vashti. She has been instantly deposed when she refused to parade her charms before the king's friends. And Esther must have known that her physical beauty had a lot to do with her selection as a successor. There had been no written test, only an all night interview. But she seemed relatively safe in her position as long as she stayed in shape and did not get out of line. Or so it seemed.

The day of testing finally came for her. Her people were about to be persecuted and executed because of the hatred of Haman, a minister of government. Only she could possibly get to the king to ask for mercy. But to approach the king unbidden was to risk death. To do nothing was to fail the great challenge of her life. Her Uncle Mordecai wrote to her: "Do not suppose that, because you are in the king's palace, you are going to be the one Jew to escape . . . Who knows? Perhaps you have come to the throne for just such a time as this" (Esth 4:13-14, *Jerusalem Bible*).

Esther accepted the challenge and saved her people. But before she approached the king (and possibly her death), she prayed the prayer of a human alone and frightened before the great challenge of life:

> My Lord, our King, the only one,
> come to my help, for I am alone
> and have no helper but you
> and am about to take my life in my hands.
> Give me courage and come to my help, for I am alone
> and have no one but you, Lord.
> Save me from my fear (see Esth 4:17L, 17R, 17T, 17Z).

Esther was queen of all that she surveyed, but this did not protect her from the day she had to "take her life in her hands" and face the future bravely. It did not save her from the fear and isolation that is so often part of such moments. There was no escape from responsibility for one's life, not even for a queen of the world.

I must remember that truth: days of trial and challenge must certainly come. I must not become so attached to the things and people that I have now that I am unwilling to move on with my life if the Lord calls me. I must not be so attached to this life that I fear to move through death to the life that is ahead. When I am tempted to place my treasure in the here and now, I must remember the words St. Augustine wrote to a friend:

> This is indeed a dying life, whatever mortal comfort it may shower on us, whatever companions may share it with us. I am certain that you recognize how temporary all these things are. . . . A human being lives a life defined by the things loved, by the things desired, by the things thought to bring happiness. . . . The only thing, my friend, that we ought to seek without reservation in this life is to be forever in the arms of the Lord *(Letter 130).*

Bishop Augustine recognized the same truth perceived by Queen Esther on her day of challenge. The essential choice for any human being is the choice between the things of time and the things of eternity. Every human must face that choice. Even being a queen is no escape.

Friday of the First Week: Dismas

Our ways are certainly *not* the ways of the Lord. For that we can be thankful! Because the Lord is in charge, we can be certain that past evils can be forgiven. We can leave past indiscretions behind us. They need not warp our future. At the same time the little good that we do is never forgotten. The Lord never forgets the tiny good things that we do, because he can see his reflection in each and every one of them.

It would be quite different if we were in charge. We remember evil and forget good. If a marriage fails, we remember the pain at the end, not the good at the beginning. If a priest or religious fails, we remember the failure more than the good done previously. It seems sometimes that every good act is done in secret. Even our most public virtues are quickly forgotten. Our most private vices, however, seem to be forever remembered by our fellow humans. Perhaps it is the burden of original sin that we cannot seem to allow each other to make even one mistake. It is so hard for us to forgive each other! And it is almost impossible for us to forget!

It is not so with the Lord, thank God! The story of Dismas proves that. Dismas was the so-called "good" thief. He died with Jesus on Calvary. Just before he died, he asked for mercy, and Jesus replied: "This day you shall be with me in paradise." Dismas was thus the first human being to get into heaven. Imagine, a thief! Perhaps Jesus wanted this good thief in heaven first so that he could take the tickets at the door from the rest of us trying to get in. Dismas would be a good choice for the admissions office. A thief is not likely to be haughty or surprised upon seeing the riffraff who show up among the saved. After his last minute rescue Dismas could ill afford to complain that others saved by the skin of their teeth (and the Blood of the Lord) were lowering neighborhood standards. He, above all, could understand the importance of that last question asked by the Lord of every human facing death: "Do you want to come with me *now*? Do you *now*, at the moment of your death, love me more than the rest?"

We do not know if Dismas did anything good in his life before his last hours. Whatever went before, by a grace of coincidence and conversion he was in the physical presence of the suffering Jesus, he felt sympathy for him, and finally he came to believe and hope in him. That was enough to save him. Of course his miracle of salvation would be even more extraordinary if that was the only good thing he had ever done. Usually we humans die as we have lived. If we have never tried to reach beyond ourselves in our days of strength, it is unlikely that we shall do so in our last moment. Still, it is possible and if through some miracle we are able to turn our attention to the Lord at the end, that is enough. If we have fixed our attention on God, or at least have fixed our attention on the place where we think God may be, or at the *very least* have wanted to fix our attention on some God, some savior, some lover of infinite capacity and understanding, perhaps that will be enough for the Lord to come to us with his salvation. Perhaps that crack in our normally self-centered life will give him the chance to break through and save us with his healing grace.

Such last minute salvation is not fair. We certainly do not deserve it. But if God gives it, who will complain? Certainly not Dismas. The possibility of such last minute salvation is demonstrated by his life. His life and death teaches that we must never give up on ourselves, because the Lord never does. No matter what we have done, the Lord is waiting for us now to make even the faintest move in his direction. Dismas says, "Donald, never give up! You can find the Lord even on that last cross of life, your death."

It is a consoling thought, indeed, as I rush along towards resurrection. But I must be careful of presumption. I must not presume that I will meet the Lord at the end even though I have ignored him from the beginning. There were two humans who died with Jesus that day, and the other thief died cursing the unfairness of it all. Hopefully he was covered by the Lord's last prayer: "Father, forgive them; they do not know what they are doing" (Luke 23:34a). We know that Dismas was saved. We do not know if the other thief accepted the Lord. Only the Lord knows. And only he knows whether the life of any human is worthy of reward or punishment.

I must remember that when I am tempted to gossip about the lives of others. I have enough to worry about in trying to take care of my own.

Saturday of the First Week: Chasms

There are great chasms in our lives that can be bridged only by love. I look around my present life and see separations from other humans. I look ahead and see the chasm of death separating me from what I have now and what shall be. I say to my human loves and to my Lord: "My friend, I am here and you are there. How can I bridge the gap?" St. Paul (and Jesus) answer: "Only by love" (1 Cor 12-13).

Love is the only bridge on which I can cross my future death with confidence and peace. Paul says that at the end of my life there will be only three things of lasting value: my faith, my hope, and my love of the Lord. Love is the greatest, because it alone will go with me across the chasm of death. It alone will be the force that will draw me irresistibly into the next life. Just as my love draws me home after a long and tiresome trip, so will it draw me across death to the loves that wait for me on the other side. On the other side of death, I will no longer need faith because I shall *see*. I will no longer need hope because I shall *possess*. Only love will remain, and it will go on growing forever.

Is this just pious jargon? Hardly! It is the promise of the Lord. It is as real as the humanity and divinity of the Lord. Even now the promise is not beyond facts of my own earthly experience. Even now I have the experience of love drawing me out of myself to distant places. Left to myself, I would live only here and only now. I would perish sitting stolidly in my present, because all my "presents" perish. To live I must move beyond them, and it is my love that moves me. In my heart I live wherever my loves live. In my heart I live in past precious moments of holding them. In my heart I live in future possibilities of seeing them again. When I love someone who is not here just now, I lean towards that future when we shall be together again. When I am far away from the one I love, I live each moment in that distant treasured place that holds them.

Can I truly love someone who is far away? Yes indeed! I do so every day. Some of my loves live in distant places. Some of my loves have gone across the chasm of death before me. I no longer can see many of my distant loves, but I am warmed by memories. I am comforted by dreams of them. I look forward to being with them again someday. I know that I have not lost my absent loves, because the ache of their absence throbs in my every here and every now.

But what about someone I have never seen? How can I love them? How can I love someone who has never spoken to me personally? How can I love someone who has never touched me? Is such love pure fantasy? Is such love more akin to hope? It is a crucial question for me as I rush towards resurrection. I must cross the chasm of death first, and only the love of the Lord can carry me across that space beyond time. And I have never *seen* the Lord.

There is a saying among the skeptical that "seeing is believing." Perhaps it is true that you always do believe in what you see. It is certainly not true that seeing and loving are so intimately connected. We do not always love those we see. It is not unknown that humans can sit *alone* in a crowded room, separated from each other by chasms of indifference or hate or suspicion or fear. On the other hand, I have sat in solitary study rejoicing in the affection of those I can no longer see. Love is not seeing. Love is choosing, and I can choose and be chosen even though separated by space and time from my love.

I need not *see* in order to love my loves. But I must *know* them. I cannot love what I do not know. Thus to love the Lord, I must somehow know him. Is this possible? Is it possible that "believing is knowing," that there is a type of knowledge that comes through faith? It would seem to be the case even on the earthly level. I can be inspired by the feats of an Abraham Lincoln and by the words of a St. Augustine. Even on the natural level I can come to know the reality of the man, Jesus Christ. I can know that he claimed to be more than a man. I can know that he died a terrible death. I can know that he promised that a human who believed in him would conquer death. I can know all these claims and these promises even on the purely natural level of knowledge. And then in some mysterious way through the grace of God, I can come to believe that all these claims and promises are true. I can know more about Jesus than I do about the hundreds of humans I see every day. I can love more this distant Lord than the stranger I pass in the corridor. But I must choose to love him. I must choose to pay attention to him, just as I must choose to pay attention to and love my human loves. In practicing my love on them (especially when they are far away), I practice loving the unseen Lord who is right next to me.

I know that I must die, and I am afraid. The distance between this life and the next seems so great! The Lord has told me not to be afraid. He promises that his love will catch me on the other side of death. Perhaps if I practice leaping the chasms that separate me from my human loves, I will bravely leap that great chasm at the end of my life. Love is the bridge.

Second Sunday: The One Who Was Left Behind

The story is told that once Jesus took time off from his rush to resurrection to go on a trip with friends. He took three of them up on a mountain where he showed them what was hidden under the grime of his humanity. Peter, James, and John saw Jesus Christ as he truly is: Jesus-God. After the vision the three of them and Jesus came back down to their usual lives in the world below.

Those who had been left behind (people like Thomas) must have allowed themselves a moment of unchristian glee when they saw the vacationers returning as tired and grimy and unsanctified as ever. Those who had been left behind, like Thomas, must have been relieved to see that Jesus had come back to them. For a time they may have worried that they had missed the boat. Thomas, for one, always seemed to be doing that. For example he was the one who was out of the room when Jesus appeared after his resurrection. Thomas was like the kid who always missed the bus for summer camp. Thomas was like those poor souls who always seem to drive others to the airport for fun vacations in Hawaii, but never get to go themselves. Thomas always seemed to be in the wrong place at the wrong time. He was always too tied down by the business life to enjoy any new adventure.

Thus he was not on hand when the invitations were given out to take a day off and to go to the mountain. When he heard that Peter, James, and John were going with Jesus, he may have smiled and said, "Have a nice day!" But deep down inside he may have hoped that their day would not be *too* good. He certainly hoped that they did not come back with a lot of slides. Home movies are the ultimate affront to those who have to stay behind. I would not be surprised if Thomas *did* not stew in the juice of sour grapes. It was not noble but so what? He was *steamed*! Jesus seemed more interested in gallivanting with a few favored souls on the heights than caring for the poor slugs trapped in the valley. Thomas was hurt at being left behind.

Thus he must have felt a special joy when he saw his friends coming back to him unchanged. He felt the joy of the kid whose mother took his sister, not him, into the store and then saw his sister returning with no new toy and no new joy. Seeing his friends returning no better from their vacation must have reassured him that he was not loved any less because he had not been taken along. It seemed to demonstrate that the reality of life with Jesus is not in ecstasy on foreign mountains but in getting through ordinary days in the familiar valleys of one's life.

Of course Thomas was completely mistaken about the purpose of the trip to the mountain. It was not meant to be a reward nor a converting experience for the three disciples. Perhaps Jesus suggested it as much for himself as for them. Perhaps he wanted to get some understanding, some affirmation from his friends, before he began his final trip to Golgotha. He certainly got little down in the valley. Perhaps the isolation of the mountain would be more conducive to facing facts. Down in the valley he was met with dazed expressions when he mentioned his death. The disciples could not understand the possibility of the Lord failing. He was their king, and they were to be his court. Perhaps Jesus went to the mountain to find someone to talk to sensibly about life and death. Perhaps he went to the mountain to find someone who would say: "Yes, I know you are going to die. I understand and I accept that. You will not be alone. I will love you in your dying as much as I have loved you in your living." Something like that seems to have happened. Luke 9:30-1 says that Moses and Elias came to Jesus and spoke to him about his death. And the Father affirmed him in his dying, saying: "This is my beloved son in whom I am well pleased." Perhaps the reason was as simple as that: Jesus needed to talk to someone about his dying. Peter and James and John were invited only because they were available. Thomas could just as easily have gone if he had been in the right place when Jesus came looking. But that was not his style.

I wonder why the three men accepted the invitation? They were more comfortable on the sea than on the heights. No great promises were made to them. They were offered only a day slightly different from the ordinary. Sometimes that is enough. When things are not going right, any chance for a change is attractive. Peter may have had another argument with his wife. He always seemed to be going away at the wrong time. Perhaps his mother-in-law was sick again, and Peter was burdened by her complaints about his never being around when he was needed. If things are hot at home, going to a mountain is a good chance to let things cool down. Perhaps James and John were trying to get over being "passed over" for good jobs in the kingdom. They could not understand what Jesus meant by his suggestion that they had to "work" for their place in heaven. Going to a mountain is not bad therapy for someone who has just been told to "go and fly a kite." Perhaps that was the message heard by James and John in Jesus' refusal to make them princes.

For whatever reason, the three men accepted the invitation to go to the mountain with Jesus. They climbed and panted up the steep hill, and upon reaching the top they promptly fell asleep. Jesus went off to pray. After a time he returned. He shook them awake, and for an instant they saw the glory of Jesus-God. Then it was over. They made their slow way back down into the deepening darkness of the valley below. They carried a memory, but like all memories it was easily buried in the troubles of everyday life. The memory did not make it any easier for them to stay faithful. It did not slow Peter and James as they fled from Jesus in Gethsemane.

The four travelers arrived back from their trip quite late. Jesus may have called out to those left behind: "We are back!" Thomas may have rolled over in his sleep and mumbled: "Thank God for that! Tomorrow will be a long day." He spoke the truth, for on the morrow Jesus was to begin his trip to Jerusalem and to his death.

Monday of the Second Week: Kindly Dumb

Marking philosophy papers, I sometimes get depressed at good people constantly coming up with dumb answers. They cannot tell their essence from their existence. If they come up with a good definition of substance, it is only by accident. And even more depressing is the realization that they could spend the rest of their lives dedicated to the study of philosophy and get no better at it. And yet many of them seem to be able to go on living. They may even make others glad to be alive. They cannot understand philosophy, but they know how to be kind. Through that precious gift they meet Jesus Christ.

It is a fact of life that we cannot all be smart. But there is no reason why we cannot be kind. Being kind is more important. When Jesus was instructing his disciples he did not command, "Be smart!" He said: "Be compassionate. . . . Do not judge. . . . Do not condemn. . . . Pardon. . . . Give, and it shall be given to you. Good measure pressed down, shaken together, running over, will they pour into the fold of your garment. For the measure you measure with will be measured back to you" (Luke 6:36-8). What is being measured? Not smart answers but kind deeds.

We are all expected to be kind because we all can be kind. Smartness is a matter of how well the intellect works. Smartness is no guarantee of holiness. We can be as smart as the devil and not be wise. Wisdom depends more on how the human being works than on how the mind works. The young St. Augustine was smart, but the uneducated St. Monica was wise. We humans are social (beings made for love), and thus it is essential for us to be kind to each other if we are to reach perfection. Indeed, we need kindness just to get by in our daily life. We hurt each other more by our unkindness than by our dumbness. No one dies with a smile simply because they think they have discovered the meaning of being.

Many have died easily, because in their last days they are touched by kindness. If I am dumb, I may not be able to help you too much, but if I am kind, I will never hurt you too much.

Does God come to the smart? Sometimes he does. He came to St. Augustine but only when he was thirty-three. Why did the conversion take so long? Because St. Augustine was so tied up in himself and his pleasures and his dreams that he had no room for anyone else. St. Augustine was smart from the beginning. Only later in life did he become unselfish. God made him kind and then came to him with the grace to persevere.

God always comes to the kind. This is clear in the conversation Jesus had with his disciples one day:

> "Anyone who loves me will be true to my word, and my Father will love him; we will come to him and make our dwelling place with him" (John 14:23).

("But how shall I know that I love you, Lord?")

> 'Love one another as I have loved you" (John 15:12).

("And how do you love me, Lord?")

> "You are my friends" (John 15:14).

The message is clear: if we are friends to one another, that is, are kind, we will come to love Jesus too. And when we are truly friends with Jesus, God will live with us forever.

And thus, my friend, you should rejoice that you are kind. Your salvation is assured. Do not worry that you are dumb; just do not take my philosophy class.

Tuesday of the Second Week: The River

Now in the midstream of my life, I pray: "Give light to my eyes that I may not sleep in death lest my enemy say, 'I have overcome him' " (Ps 13:4-5). Now is the time to take charge of my life and control its flow. I must look at it and see it as the Lord sees it. I must get his perspective. I must talk it over with him. I must accept his invitation: "Come now, let us set things right" (Isa 1:18). I must fight the temptation to float along with this moment's currents. I must not sleep away my life lest I fall into that infinite second sleep that so frightened St. Augustine, that eternal darkness where I am separated from my loves. I must now, in this symbolic second week that marks my days of strength and possibility, see my life as it really is and take charge.

Long ago, Heraclitus, a Greek wise man, wrote that every human life is like a river rushing towards the sea. He did not know that the sea was infinite nor that we are rushing towards resurrection, but he was right in his understanding that we humans are constantly on the move, that we are carried along irresistibly into our future, that we cannot step twice into any moment of our lives. My life flows into the future. What am I to make of that? I may be tempted to sit back and simply float along. Death is inevitable. Why bother trying to direct my life?

Jesus gives the answer, and his message is clear. I am called not to peace but to struggle. That I shall live for a while and then die and then live again, this future is fixed. But whether I shall live a decent life now, whether I shall die with no regrets, whether I shall rise gloriously to find love, these are issues yet to be settled. They can only be settled by me with the help of the Lord. The quality of my life and death and life thereafter depends on whether I now take responsibility for my life and fight bravely against the currents that would rip me away from that sparkling rushing stream that leads to the infinite sea.

I am part of the human river rushing towards resurrection. Like every river there seem to be parts that lose the way. Some water wanders off into dead eddies where it becomes stagnant. It becomes a place of rottenness. It reflects the truth of Heraclitus' somber statement: "Souls smell in Hades." There are other waters which lose the way despite their best efforts to find the main course. They do not give up. They find new ways around the obstacles that divert them, splashing bravely against the huge rocks that block their path, leaping vigorously down great falls, making rainbows as they try to hold light in their lives. If they do not tire, they will finally find their way back to the main current and with it plunge proudly into the limitless sea, leaving a broad path far out on its surface, the mark of a life well lived, of a course well run.

The difference between human life and a river is that in life there is no escape from the eternal sea. Even the stagnant pools, the places where water has lost its way and given up the search, come to the sea eventually. The dead water evaporates and is carried to infinity. Slowly, ever so reluctantly, it passes the boundary of its time and meets forever. Its muddied, sullied drops reach the eternal sea to become part of a strange polluted cell, a deadly place in the midst of an ocean teeming with infinite life.

Heraclitus saw this too. He said that the sea into which the river of human life empties is composed of waters most pure and waters most foul. Where I shall be depends on what I do now. Now in the midstream of my life, it is time to stop floating with the passing currents. It is time to take charge of my life and, with the help of the Lord, to join that rushing river that speeds towards his eternal embrace.

Wednesday of the Second Week: Getting Ahead

Many of us seem to be driven by a need to get ahead. We are too busy to live and too busy to die. We want to "make something of ourselves," and we will do almost anything to achieve that goal. We worry if we think we are not getting ahead as fast as we should. When anyone is chosen over us, we become sad. We cannot muster the humility of John the Baptist saying: "He must increase: I must decrease," a prophecy dramatically fulfilled by Christ gaining a cross and John losing a head. The paradox of the Baptist's life (and every human life for that matter) was that it substantially improved only when he died. He finally got ahead when he lost his head.

It is in light of the common human passion to be successful that we must understand that odd incident in the New Testament story when we discover the disciples John and James sending their mother to plead with Jesus for better jobs in the kingdom (Matt 20: 17-28). The first thing that must be said about the event is that it proves that the whole family was cursed with bad timing. Jesus had just finished telling the world that he soon was to be arrested, beaten, and finally executed. It was not a good time for his employees to ask for a raise. But we must not be too hard on James and John. The other disciples seem no less insensitive. They were indeed angry when they heard of the petition, but there is no indication that their fury was prompted by concern for Jesus. They were mad because they had not thought of the stratagem first. All of them seemed more concerned about "getting ahead" than about the imminent death of their Lord.

How do we explain such apparent callousness? A charitable explanation would be to suggest that the whole bunch was so convinced about universal immortality that the death of a loved one was no problem for them. Perhaps they thought of death as no more serious a matter than falling asleep. Certainly there is nothing wrong in asking the boss for a raise knowing that he is soon going to take a nap. However, if the disciples had such noble indifference to death, it did not last very long. On the night before Jesus' death, they seemed terribly scared of death.

A more likely explanation for their insensitivity is simply this: at that moment in their lives they were so dominated by the need to get ahead that they had no room for anything else. They heard only what they wanted to hear, and they wanted to hear nothing that was unrelated to their future prospects. They wanted to get ahead. They had no time to hear of death. Like so many of us who are still worried about getting along in life, they had little time for those whose life was apparently over. Their present was too promising to worry about the future. They did not want to listen to anyone who was approaching death lest they be distracted from their careers.

Jesus did not seem upset by their lack of feeling. He understood human passion. He knew that the desperate desire of humans *to be something* flowed from their primordial condition of being nothing. Moreover, he did not want to dissuade them from ambition. He did not want to create the impression that it was unchristian to do a little work sometimes. The human passion to do nothing is just as destructive as the passion to accomplish everything. Thus Jesus did not want to say that work was a sin. This was the message he gave to Zacchaeus the businessman (Luke 19:1-10). He did not condemn him for working. He suggested that he take some time off to talk with God. In his conversation Jesus may have told Zacchaeus that it was not ungodly to make a dollar as long as the dollar was not made Almighty God. As far as we know, Zacchaeus went back to the office after his day off with Jesus. The difference may have been only this: after talking with Jesus, Zacchaeus did not believe that his career was the most important thing in his life.

Thus Jesus was not upset that John and James (or Donald and you) wanted to make something of themselves. He only worried that they (and we) would forget that we are rushing towards resurrection and that ultimate success is in being loved by God.

Thursday of the Second Week: Mixed Signals

St. Augustine was of the opinion that the two major effects of original sin are a tendency to make bad choices and a tendency to be simply dumb. Not only do we choose to do what we should not do, we also do not have a clear idea of what we should do. Our practical dumbness flows from our lack of understanding of the way things are, of the way other people are, of the way *we* are. God's words through the mouth of Jeremiah are aimed at each one of us: "The human heart is more devious than any other thing, perverse too: who can pierce its secrets? I alone probe the mind and test the heart." (Jer 17:9-10).* The Lord alone seems to be able to understand what we humans are trying to say to each other, what we are trying to say to him, and what we are trying to say to ourselves. We humans live and die in a world of mixed signals.

Our trouble with truth is that it is sometimes hard to bear and hard to say. Thus when we must say hard truths to each other, we often begin with vague hints. The words, "Miss Jones is not available just now," sometimes mean that a great romance has cooled. Being left with no assignment when those around us are busy may be a sign that our working days are numbered. A tinge of anxiety deep down inside my heart may be a sign that my life is not in good order.

We must be sensitive to such soft signals when they first occur. They speak gently of harsh facts, and if we recognize their meaning early, we are better prepared for the brave response that they demand. Knowing early that our life is changing can prevent us from being terribly hurt when we are let go by a love or a boss. Knowing from the beginning that we have the same weaknesses as every other human being can prevent us from becoming involved in a maelstrom of passion that destroys our time and eternity.

We would never become addicted to a potion or a person if we turned away at the first hint of danger. In the beginning no one

*The first sentence is from the Jerusalem Bible, the second from the New American Bible.

is addicted to that which eventually destroys. In time the addiction grows and overcomes the suffering it causes. We cannot stop even though our actions threaten to destroy us and the ones we love. How much better would it be if we had the sense to respond to that first signal from nature, that first signal from our love, that first signal from our conscience, telling us that we must change our lives because we are not living the truth.

Often we do not change our ways in time. We do not listen, or we do not try to understand the signal that is being sent. Indeed, we *will* not listen even when the truth is being shouted at us by the circumstances of our lives. Reality shouts at us, and we cannot seem to hear. No wonder that we do not hear when the first hints of changing times come to us:

> when a close friend suddenly stops calling us and is very businesslike and appropriately polite when we call to find out what happened; when a soul mate with whom we have spent a lifetime hints that she is dying by her disinterest in ordinary affairs and by the sudden quietness in her face.

We get mixed signals, and our need to make things better than they are blots out the truth from our lives.

Jesus knows the problem. Through his whole life he had to deal with people who were always missing the point. From the very beginning of his public life, he tried to tell his disciples that their lives would not be made any easier by following him. He tried to make it plain to them that he had no intention of becoming a king of this world nor would they be his princes. He told them as clearly as he could that his destiny in this life was to be executed. He tried to tell them that someday they would die too. But they did not hear him, because they did not want to hear him. They would not listen to the Lord telling them that he would be considered to be an earthly failure by people of his time. They would not hear words of his failure, because they said that they would be earthly failures too, and they had no other prospects.

If only they had listened to Jesus, perhaps they would have been better prepared for his death. Perhaps Mark would not have run away naked. Perhaps Peter would not have denied him. Perhaps

Judas would not have taken his own life. If they had not gotten mixed signals, perhaps the disciples would have enjoyed their days with the Lord and with their loves even more. If they had listened better, if they had accepted the truth of their times better, perhaps they would have lived better. Perhaps the same can be said of you and me as we make our way down the road towards resurrection.

Friday of the Second Week: Prayers for Different Ages

The story of Israel and his sons tells me important things about being old and being young on this road to resurrection. Genesis tells us that "Israel loved Joseph best of all his sons, for he was the child of his old age" (Gen 37:3). Israel's special love is not surprising. Sometimes we cherish more the accomplishments of later life. They are testimony to the fact that in our final days we have not lost the knack of making a mark on life, of being important, of being worthy of respect and love. When we are young, we do not relish our victories as much. We are too anxious to get on to the next adventure. When we are old, we are not quite sure that there will be a new adventure. Perhaps that is why we are so sad at losing our loves in later years. We are not sure that we will have time to find a new one. We are not sure that we can muster the energy to even look. Israel was destroyed when Joseph disappeared, because Joseph was his *last* son. The production line had closed down.

The story also tells us about the envy that the old have for the young. It says: "When his brothers saw that their father loved him best of all his sons, they hated him so much that they would not even greet him" (Gen 37:4). The degree of displeasure may seem extravagant, but the fact of displeasure should be understood by anyone who has ever been passed over for someone younger. No one likes to be second best. No one likes to be traded in for a younger model. When the old are discarded, they may feel that their only future is the junkyard. Though we do not like to admit it, there comes a time in life when we are beyond the possibility of cosmetic recalls. As we become craggy beyond repair, we are tempted to believe that our best days are behind us, and we envy those who still seem to be enjoying them. Of course the envy is silly. There is no best age. Every age has its own fears and its own needs. Every age has its appropriate prayer.

I must remember that as I am swept through my times to eternity. I am indeed like the grass which springs up in the morning. When I was in the morning of life, I grew quickly and flowered easily (though sometimes with weed blossoms). Now in the evening my early blossoms necessarily fade. When I was in the morning of my life, everything seemed possible. I dreamt of blooming forever, and I prayed the prayer of the young, the prayer of those just beginning great ventures:

> In the morning fill with love and then we shall
> laugh and sing forever.
> Give us joys to blot out our afflictions
> on the days when misfortune strikes us.
> You have made us, O God! Give us success! (see Ps 90:14-17).

When I was young I dreamt of a perfect love who would be with me as I conquered the world. I prayed, "Give me love! Give me success!" But now my prayer has become more simple. I pray: "Make me know the shortness of life that I may gain wisdom of heart" (Ps 90:12).

My prayer now is not sad; it is just realistic. In the evening of my life, I know that I am loved but I also know that my love cannot be imprisoned. I cannot grasp my human loves too tightly as we move towards resurrection. I must be prepared to let them go. I will always love them. This I know. But I cannot possess them until my now becomes forever. I pray now not that I shall find love but that my loves shall ever be happy, that someday we shall embrace in the arms of the Lord.

As for success, I no longer pray for it the way I used to. Now I know that I will never be secure in success until I love and am loved forever. I know now that this will not happen until I wake from the sleep of death to find my divine and human loves waiting for me.

When I was young, I needed many things and prayed for many things. I wanted to make a mark in this life. I wanted to find love. I wanted to experience joy. Now that I am older, my prayer is to see my life as the Lord sees it. With that vision I would be able to see that my life is a road without end, a road in which "a thousand years . . . are as yesterday, now that it is past, or as a watch of the night" (Ps 90:4).

In the midst of such an eternal life, it is silly to be sad about being young or about being old. There are no second class citizens on the road to resurrection. The conditions are the same for all. We are all being carried along at equal speed. The differences between us are miniscule when compared with the limitless life beyond death. On the days when I am convinced of that, I have the wisdom that was given to Solomon: "I have an understanding heart" (see 1 Kings 3:7-12).

Saturday of the Second Week: Prodigal Sons

The story of the Prodigal Son (Luke 15:1-32) teaches important lessons about this life and the next. It teaches that God (symbolized by the father in the story) is always prepared to take us back when we wander away. All we need do is ask forgiveness and come back home. The story also teaches a rule for large families: when you kill a fatted calf for one kid you are certain to get the other kids' goat. Even the best of families has its tensions.

This is not saying that loving someone is not a great boon. Being born into a loving family and perhaps having a family of one's own—daughters and sons of one's flesh and blood—can be a source of great joy. When everything goes well, when everyone is healthy and happy, when no one is mixed up, when everyone lives long and fruitful lives, when everyone really cares about each other and proves it in action, in sum, when everything is just fine, family living can be a source of great happiness. But when things are not so fine, there can be great pain.

When we lose a loved one through death or misunderstanding or just plain indifference, the pain is greater than if we had never had love at all. When we lose a love, we know what we are missing. If we never had the love, we do not know what we have missed. Though both states are sad, sometimes the latter is the less painful. When we lose a love, when our love turns their back on us, we need great courage and hope. We need to believe that we shall see again those who have died before us. We need to believe that we shall someday understand why those who once seemed to love us suddenly rejected us. We need to believe that someday we shall understand the sometimes strange paths that our loved ones take in pursuit of the Lord. Our faith may help us to be convinced that someday we shall know and understand and possess our wandering loves. The day will come when we shall no longer worry about them or be disappointed in them or be rejected by them. Someday everything will be just fine between us and our loves, but just now we feel like punching them in the mouth.

That is what I feel like doing to the two boys in the story. They make me mad. The poor father has my sympathy. He had large estates, great numbers of cattle, and two jackasses—both of them sons. Neither of his boys was much of a prize. One never grew up, and the other could not wait for the old man to die so that he could inherit a wealth he had never earned. Looking at the situation as an outsider, my advice to the father would be threefold:

1. Send a shovel to the son on the dunghill with the message, "Get to work!"
2. Inform your other son that you intend to spend all of your hard earned wealth before you die and that all you will leave him will be a carefully worked wall plaque with the fond message: "I got mine; now you get yours!"
3. Then go to Bermuda for some great fishing.

God says that he will not act that way towards us. He says that he will be like the father in the story, forgiving and patient. God does not get mad at prodigals nor call them bad names like we do. And we can thank God for that!

Third Sunday: The Alien

Now in the midst of my life, I suddenly feel as though I do not belong. Perhaps someone would say that it is midlife crisis. I believe that it is no crisis at all. It is an awakening to the contingency of my life. It is a realization that my desire for self-sufficiency, my desire for solutions, and my desire to have everything perfect are desires that cannot be fulfilled just now. My feeling of strangeness now in my midlife is nothing more than an understanding that I am wounded and in need of healing. There is nothing particularly wrong in my life. There is no place here where my life will be any less strange. I am alienated only because I am an alien and I shall remain so until I finally go home.

The story of Jesus and the Samaritan woman at the well (John 4:5-42) has a hopeful message for us human aliens. It says: "Jesus comes to aliens too." We may be separated from our home, but we are never separated from our Lord. This message is of special importance to me in midcourse of my rush to resurrection. In the middle of this life, the feeling of not belonging can become especially strong. There is a growing feeling of uncertainty, of restlessness, of not being in control of one's situation. The unease can take many forms. I realize that my employment has ceased to be a career and has become only a job. I may see that I do not possess my loved ones, that they have other interests, other concerns, loves other than me. I may have the feeling that I am only a visitor in the life of my love, sharing room with many others. I seem to have disappeared from the view of those I am with. They see me physically, but I have no impact on their lives. I am like a man in a strange city waiting for a light to change. I stand in the midst of a crowd almost touching and yet distanced, because we are not each other's kind. We share space but not lives. I am an alien in another's place.

I am consoled by the thought that just as Jesus wanted to be with the alien Samaritan woman, so he may want to be with me in my foreign place. The woman was alien because she was both Samaritan and woman. Thus she was truly amazed that Jesus would pay any attention to her at all. She asked: "How is it that you, a Judean, ask for a drink from me, a Samaritan woman?" (see John 4:9). Judeans looked down on Samaritans generally. And even within the Samaritan nation women were not the usual bearers of great gifts or important messages. Thus it was unexpected that the Lord would come to the Samaritans through a woman. She was an alien in her own town, and once she had brought the message of Jesus to them, they denied that she had done much at all. They said: "We don't need *you* to teach us about Jesus. We believe on our own!"

If her public life bore the mark of the alien, so too did her private life. She had had five husbands, a sure sign of one who has loved and lost. She had been a stranger in her own house. She had suffered personal rejection four times. And yet with all of that, she seemed to live with humor and hope. She was still taking water from the well for another day's living. She was not yet jumping into wells to end it all. Though she had been disappointed in her friends, she was not frightened of conversation with a stranger. She was not reticent in sharing her life with a foreigner who seemed to be interested in her. She was willing to accept a Savior who came to her in alien garb. She accepted her distance from the "good life" without disgust or despair. She still was able to talk to a God she could not see.

St. Augustine, whose own life was powerfully affected by strong women, recommended to his Christian people that they see themselves in this alien woman. He told them:

> The fact that she came from a foreign people is part of the symbolic meaning, for she is a symbol of the Church. We must then recognize ourselves in her words and in her person and with her give our own thanks to God for the living water that the Lord is willing to give to all the thirsty, even those who are at a great distance from him (*Treatises on The Gospel Of John* 15:10-12).

When I feel like an alien, I must remember that the Lord came to aliens to save them. And this he did by dying for them. I must remember the words that Paul wrote to those foreigners, the Romans: "At the appointed time, when we were still powerless, Christ died for us godless men. . . . It is precisely in this that God proves his love for us: that while we were still sinners, Christ died for us" (Rom 5:6, 8).

Monday of the Third Week: Separations

There is a true saying that "You can't go home again!" It reflects the special burden of being a human being constantly on the move. We are constantly leaving lovingly remembered places and people. Kids leave home. Brothers and sisters separate. Great loves are torn apart by changing places and changing lives. Sometimes it happens that you are able to return to old places lovingly remembered, but they are never the same. The people are the same but yet different. You left as an intimate and now return as a visitor. You perceive that you now have a low priority in the lives of those with whom you once shared a love. It is no use being upset by it. It is just the way life goes for a people rushing down individual paths towards resurrection.

Jesus knew the experience. As he was about to begin his great mission in life, he returned to the town of his youth (Luke 4:16ff). He discovered that if anyone thought of him at all, they thought of him only as that little carpenter's son who had left town some time before. For them he was still the kid on the corner. He could not be taken seriously as a teacher. If he had come back offering to mend their tables, they would have understood. They could not accept his offer to mend their lives. He was a stranger to them. They resented him in the same way that a small town resents the college freshman who returns on his first vacation spouting all the answers to life to his poor dumb friends left behind. Jesus had left town, and when he returned he discovered that he was a stranger.

There is nothing unusual in this. It truly takes great effort to maintain intimacy over space and time. More often than not it begins to fade. It is a rude shock to find that former intimates are more concerned about their present life than their former love. We remember fondly the days when we had shared lives, when there was not enough time to talk about all the things we wanted to talk about, when we gave and received the big and little events in our daily lives. We anticipate with joy renewing the acquaintance, picking up where we left off, holding hearts as we once did so long ago. It is a rude awakening to discover that all we can say are those polite trivialities usually reserved for passing acquaintances. At one time we seemed to share each second, but now we ask, "What's new?" and respond, "Nothing much!" and go on about more important business. Separateness has made lovers like distant ships passing in the night, signaling each other across the sea by sterile and neutral crackling sounds. They are trying to make their way to safe harbors, but now by distant paths. There can be great pain in such experience if we honestly believe that absence would make hearts grow fonder. There is great foolishness if we try desperately to take up our old place in the lives of our old loves. Old wines are obnoxious when they become too intrusive, when they knock too insistently on the lives of past loves. It is better by far to shrug one's shoulders and say: "That's life!"

Jesus' rejection did not destroy him, but it was sad. He may have only wanted to relax for a while with old friends. He may have only wanted to have a little fun before he started his work: to shoot some baskets with old classmates, to go to the beach, to sit quietly over coffee with a dear friend. But when he arrived home, he discovered that he was a stranger. He wanted to have a little holiday and ended up in the Holiday Inn, the place for people passing through.

When he tried to tell old friends his new message of hope and salvation, they hated him as a stranger who came from distant places to mess up their lives. They attacked him for forcing himself on their agenda, an agenda that had long since ceased to include him.

The story tells us that Jesus did not make a fuss. He passed by them and went about the business of the rest of his life. And so must we when we experience the strangeness of returning to past familiar places. Our past loves do not hate us. They have simply moved on as we have moved on. Perhaps someday we shall meet in love again. In the meantime we must wish them well and get on with life.

Tuesday of the Third Week: Forgiveness

In our rush to resurrection, there are few things we can control. We cannot determine when we shall be conceived or when we shall be born. We cannot determine whether we shall fall in love nor whether we shall be loved in return. We cannot determine the moment when we shall die. Sometimes we cannot control the cruel things that we do to each other. We certainly cannot forget the cruelty once done. But we can forgive, and the Lord has said that it is by the measure of the forgiveness we give that he will measure his forgiveness.

This is the clear message of his story about the servant who was forgiven a debt but would not forgive another. (Matt 18:21ff) The servant asked for charity from his lord but demanded justice from his neighbor. His unforgiving attitude was a sign that he had forgotten who he was and where he was going. It showed that he was so attached to his own few possessions that he thought them to be his forever. It showed that he wanted to dominate those who were his equal. He tried to make himself better than those who "owed" him. He forgot how much he owed for his very life, how much he owed:

> to the air that breathed him;
> to the grain that fed him;
> to the water that slaked him;
> to the earth that supported him;
> to the humans who put up with him;
> to the God who made him.

The servant's demand for unconditional justice from his fellow serv- ant showed that he wanted very much to be God. Only God has a right to say "You owe me!" But he does not say that. To be a God like the Christian God, we must be ready to say "I love you," rather than "You owe me!" To be godlike we must reflect the supreme graciousness of the infinite God who does not need cruelty to prove his superiority. The truly great one can afford to be kind. He who possesses everything will take his debtors lightly. We who have nothing, who depend on others for our very existence, have no call to take our debtors seriously, pressing them for that last ounce of blood.

This does not mean that we must be indifferent to the cruelty that is done to us or to others. This does not mean that we must be a "patsy" at the mercy of those who would take advantage of us. If the unforgiving servant in the story knew that his debtor had plenty of funds and was in the process of arranging an extended voyage around the world, he would have had a clear right to de- mand that debts be settled first. But the story does not indicate that the unforgiving servant was being used by his fellow-servant. Nor was there a need for instant repayment. The unforgiving servant had just received a great gift from his master. He could afford to give some relief to the man who owed him, and the latter had no funds socked away. He was apparently in true need. He was put in jail precisely because he did not have the money to pay. One suspects that the unforgiving servant was more interested in hurt- ing another than in getting his money.

The Lord tells us that this is a dangerous attitude for us to take towards each other. If we always demand our rights from each other, we will be in deep trouble when we come to face the Lord. His at- titude towards us will mirror the attitudes that we have taken towards each other. If we have always demanded our rights, he will give us our rights. And that is a terrifying prospect because our rights before the Lord are only these: the right to be nothing, and the right, once being something and sinful, to be damned. God help us if we get our rights! By the grace of God we shall not. We shall be treated with mercy, not justice.

St. Augustine told his people that every human is well-advised to be forgiving because every human needs forgiveness *(Sermon 144:4)*. Through our forgiveness we touch not only other humans but even Christ himself. He has identified himself with every human being. When we crucify another for a debt unpaid, we crucify the Lord again. God can forgive any sin except such unforgiving cruelty to his Son. As we rush towards resurrection the most important rule is: "Forgive each other now, so that the Lord will forgive you at the end of your days."

Wednesday of the Third Week: "Pass It On!"

As we make our way towards resurrection, there are two great fears that torture us: the fear that death is indeed the end of everything and the fear that even while alive we count for nothing much. We fear that even after a life filled with achievemnt, this poor Donald or this poor Dotty will come to death and that will be the end of *that* tune. We fear that someday we shall discover that even in our living we have been little more than a piece of junk important for nothing and to no one.

St. Augustine recognized these fears in himself and in his people. Again and again he proclaimed the response of the Lord to those fears. He thus once wrote to a friend, *"Immortality is certain!"* (*Letter 137: #12*). And to his students he proclaimed, "It is not possible to create a superfluous human being!" (*On the Freedom of the Will*, III: #26). And he insisted that these messages were not his own. His words were the words of Jesus saying to you and me, to every Donny and Dotty: "God has not made you junk, and whatever happens to you on this side of death you shall live forever." Jesus tells us that no life is a waste and that no death is a disaster. Death is another important moment in a life valued by God.

St. Augustine uses an apt apology to explain why death is so important, why it is a valued part of life. He says that death is like the last note completing the melody of our earthly lives. That last note must be sounded if our melody is to become part of the great song of the universe that God sings through all of our individual lives. The desire never to sound that last note is as silly as to wish that a great poet repeat again and again the first syllable of a great poem. Just as one syllable must die and another take its place before the melody of the poem can be appreciated, so too must our lives move from moment to moment till we reach the very end. Only at the end can the full song be heard. The great symphony of history is possible only if the individual parts come and go (*The Literal Meaning of Genesis,* I: #14). We who live now must die to give space to those yet to be conceived (*City of God,* 15:1). We must end our melody so that others can begin their tune. We must pass on the great song of our time to those who will carry it into the future.

We have a part to play, and for this reason no human life is worthless. Each plays a tune that can be carried by no one else. No one else can make the sound that we make with our unique lives. We may be only a bit of human history, but that history is a melody composed in bits and pieces. Adam, we are told, was the first bit of that "O" beginning the phrase "Once upon a time." We do not know which child yet to be conceived will be the period at the end of that story. In the meantime every tiny microdot of human life contributes to the text. We are in the middle of history's song. We are responsible for its continuity. To play our part, we must listen to those who preceded us, learn from their lives, and pass on the message to those who are to follow. Every memory we give is a message of hope or despair to those who follow. The message of Moses to the Israelites is the message of God to every human being:

> Take care and be earnestly on your guard not to forget the things which your own eyes have seen, not let them slip from your memory as long as you live, but teach them to your children and to your children's children (Deut 4:9).

I am not junk, my friend, nor are you. Each of us has a unique song to sing. And each of our songs is part of that great song that God has composed for time to sing. It is a song made up of highs and lows, of somber notes and notes of tinkling brilliance. But somber or brilliant, each note (each life) plays its part in singing the secret of existence: "God is love!"

Thursday of the Third Week: Tied Together

We become wise when we are old if we remember the past and learn from it. But wisdom in remembering can come only when you are old enough to forget. The truly important messages of the past stand out only in an environment of grace-filled forgetting. I must block out the unimportant things of my life (like what I did yesterday or what was said at last night's party) before I can productively remember. The young may say that we elders are living in the past (by trying to remember so much) because our future is so short and our arthritic present is so bleak, but why should we pay attention to such carping criticism? After all, what have they to remember? You cannot remember your school "daze" with affection when you are in the "mist" of them.

Only now when I am somewhat "long in the tooth" and "bald in the head" can I remember productively the lessons taught me in Our Lady of the Rosary Grammar School. Only now do I see that the principle for life at O.L.R. is the principle for life itself: "If you don't hang together, you will hang separately." One manifestation of this principle then was that we always traveled in packs when we went on school outings. On a field trip to the zoo, for example, we kids would be tied together in a long line. One teacher would be at the front of the line to warn the natives that we were coming. Another would take up a rearguard position to boot lollygaggers into submission. We kids were convinced at the time that the reason why we were tied together was that the administration wanted no survivors if there was some disaster. Now I can see that being tied together was a sign of love. Being tied together externally was the best protection for a gang of individuals who were not too well tied together internally. The physical regimentation of our trips protected both us and the rest of the wild beasts we met. Being tied together was the only way we could make it through school.

Now I know that it is also the only way of making it through life. This life is not always pleasant. When the dark times come, it is hard to make our way on our own. And now we are not firmly bound to each other. The only bond that ties us now is the bond of love and that knot is easily loosened. Even a slight tug of selfishness can separate us from those we love. Hurt feelings, misunderstandings, foolish passion, pride, these are the fingers that untie the knots of affection that bind us to each other. Even simple indifference causes our bonds to dry up and rot. We are left with nothing but yellowed strands of a love that once was new and strong but now is no more. To be bound to others by love needs constant care, a weaving and reweaving of our lives together. Without attention and nourishing the bond of human love is broken, and we drift apart without even realizing it.

This is truly a shame. Our human loves make happiness in this life real and happiness in the next life possible. Through our bonding with each other, we become bound to the Lord. Jesus said that he himself is present in the midst of true human love. He also said that if we are bound to him, it matters little what else happens in our life. We shall be with him forever. But to be bound, we must want to be bound. The knot of love is under our control. We can untie it whenever we wish. Jesus does not force anyone to be tied to him. He only warns that the one who is not with him is against him: "He who does not gather with me scatters" (Luke 11:23).

The Lord has done his part in bonding us to him. He has bound himself to humanity by his life and death, by his desire to live in us now through grace. But he cannot and will not force us to accept his presence. We can distract ourselves. We can spend our time chattering away about trivialities at the end of the line and become so separated from our Head that we lose him forever. We can become untied and wander off in this human zoo. No doubt he will be sorry for us. When we are missing, we will be missed. But even the Lord cannot bring us back unless we want to be brought back. Once losing the Lord, we must find him again on our own, wanting to find him first, then dredging up memories of the days when we were with him, then analyzing without excuse the reasons why we lost ourselves. Then finally we must be ready to admit humbly our sloth in being too lazy to keep up or our silliness in not being able to pay attention to the only *truly important* thing in our lives, namely, to be bound to the Lord.

During the search there is a great consolation if we remember it. The Lord is never too far away from those truly trying to find him. We are never too far off the road no matter how far we may seem to wander. We are never more than a little way from the Lord. We just cannot see him for the weeds we allow to gather around our lives. If we only cut some of them down or brush them aside, we will see him clearly. With effort we can catch up to him before our earthly excursion is over.

Of course it would be better if we never let go of his hand. But kids will be kids! We remain fickle lovers no matter how old we get. We want to be free just like the crowd at Our Lady of the Rosary did so long ago. My gang at O.L.R. was too dumb to untie the bonds that connected us; thus we survived growing up in West Philadelphia. Pray God I will not now be so dumb as to untie the bonds of love that tie me to the Lord and my friends. I can only survive with the help of my friends.

Friday of the Third Week: Peeping Out

I do not need a command to love the Lord with my whole heart and to love my neighbor as myself. I need a way. I need a way to break through the shell of selfishness that seems to trap me.

Sometimes in the dark of my nights I know the truth of that image that the real me is not the massive glob of flesh and sinew that lumbers through life only to fall apart at the end. The real me is a little fire burning brightly deep inside the mass of body that others see. Plato said that the essence of the human being was a pure spirit temporarily imprisoned in the mound of flesh we call body. Descartes described this real me as a "thinking thing" dwelling in a machine and desperately trying to see what is going on outside and make sense of it. The real me that is inside this aging mass peeps out through the bulk trying to find another flame out there with whom it can share its life. Human life is mostly a being alone within oneself, struggling to be free, trying to get beyond oneself, and touching another in love.

Sometimes in the dark of my nights, I feel the truth of this image. It is then that I need to know how to love. It is then I need someone to love. It is then that I need a friend, someone to whom I can reveal myself, someone who can truly see me through the fleshy mist that hides me. I peep out through my flesh hoping to see someone peeping back at me. I peep out through my body looking for another spirit who understands me and loves me—loves *me*, not how I look, or how I sound, or how I feel to the touch.

I dream of loving. I dream that I shall someday find that "other" to whom I can reveal what I am really like. I dream that someday someone will see through me and thereby truly see me. They will see me and pay attention to me and come to live with me deep inside this bulky body that hides me from others. I shall be able to say to them the things that for so long have been locked up inside me, what I dream, what I fear, what I regret about my past, what I hope for in my future. There deep inside I can touch a love and be touched in return. There I can be in my love and have my love in me, visiting easily back and forth in our intimacy, my flame blending with the fire that is my love. I want to touch souls, not bodies; I want to hold hearts, not hands.

But how can I? The best I seem able to do is to peep out with affection through the misting windows of my slowly sagging body. I cannot seem to touch the spirit of my loves even when I hold them in tight embrace. No matter what I do, there is always present that core of solitariness. No matter how much I reach through my flesh to some other, I seem destined to live and die by myself. No matter how hard I try, I cannot be perfectly united with my loves. Thus, I do not need a command to love; I need a way.

Jacques Maritain, that wise philosopher, said that there is no direct way to have such intimate contact with our human loves. We can reach each other only through the medium of the eternal lover. That is why Jesus insisted that we must first love God and then love our neighbor. He knew that we could not touch our neighbor completely and intimately and eternally until we were first touched by God. God alone can pierce our facade and come to that which is the real us. We do not need to fear that we will fail to do our part and thus block his passage. We do not need to understand him. We need not fear that he will not understand us. We can relax and simply rejoice that we are truly known, understood, and loved. We cannot stop his understanding of us, his seeing of us. We can only reject his love or "not pay attention" to what is happening deep inside us. We can spend so much time trying to peep out over the mountains of flesh that surround us that we ignore the one inside us who created us and died for us and who wants to be the bridge to all our human loves for all eternity.

That is the danger. I can spend so much time seeking outside loves that I ignore the lover who is even now working deep inside me. It is easy to miss him. Even St. Augustine did so for half his life. He ran this way and that searching for love. He said that he was in love with love and was in agony that he could not find satisfaction in the people or things that surrounded him. But finally he looked inside himself and found the Divine Lover, and he laughed at his silliness in wasting so much time searching the world outside for someone to come visit with him. He prayed:

Late have I loved you, O Beauty so ancient and so new!
Late have I loved you!
There you were inside me all that time when I was rushing around outside looking for you. . . .
You were here with me, but I was off someplace else, looking (*Confessions* 10:27).

Saturday of the Third Week: Simeon's Dream

When I was little I prayed the following prayer:

Now I lay me down to sleep.
I pray the Lord my soul to keep.
And should I die before I wake,
I pray the Lord my soul to take.

And then I would peacefully fall asleep. Sometimes in the dark of my nights I would get scared. Sometimes I would ride off on violent nightmares, those wild stallions of sleep that carry imagination into terrible kingdoms of fantasy. Sometimes when I was just on the edge of sleep, I would cry out in fear that I would never see the light again. In my terror I would be comforted by one who loved me. My mother or father would come and say, "Don't be afraid, my son. I shall see you on the other side of sleep. I shall see you tomorrow." Through slowly closing eyes, dulled by a day well-lived, I would see the smiles of those who loved me and would drift peacefully into sleep. I *knew* that I would rise again.

The dream of the old man Simeon was that his death would be like that. As a result of his many prayers he was promised, "You shall not see death until you have seen Christ the Lord" (see Luke 2:26). He lived many days before the promise came true. As he grew older and more feeble, he must have wondered if the promise would ever be fulfilled. He must have worried to himself: "Will I never see the Lord? Will death come and be a sleep without waking?" He must have worried sometimes as he grew older and older and saw more and more of his loves pass away, pass away without ever seeing the Lord before *they* died. But he kept his hope and his faith even as the night of death came closer and closer. Every day he hoped for and believed in and loved a Lord he had never seen. Finally the promise was fulfilled.

At the very end of his days he was in the temple, and Mary brought Jesus to him. Simeon held his Lord in his arms and rejoiced: "Now, Master, you can let your servant go in peace, . . . because my eyes have seen the salvation which you have prepared for all the nations to see" (Luke 2:29-30, *JB*). The Lord came to Simeon at the end of life, and Simeon knew peace as he went forward to embrace the dreamless sleep of death. As the shadows lengthened in his life, he *knew* that he would see the light again. He knew that he was going to die soon, but he was not afraid. He recognized the truth proclaimed later by Paul: "The life I live now is not my own; Christ is living in me" (Gal 2:20).

Simeon saw the Lord before he died and slept peacefully. Paul saw the Lord before he died (1 Cor 15:1-11) and was never again afraid of death. Why cannot the Lord come to me in the same way? Why does not the Lord come to me before my death, just as my parents would come to me before my sleep? Then surely I would sleep in death without fear. I would see the Lord before I went to that final sleep and would doze off looking forward to that new day when I would see him again. "If you did it for Simeon and Paul, Lord, why not me?"

Maybe the reason he does not come is because he knows that the sight of him would have little effect if I have not first believed in him and hoped for him and loved him. If my seeing was my first contact with him, I might say, "Who's that?" and turn away to more familiar things. Seeing Jesus is not salvation. Believing in him is. Judas saw Jesus and committed suicide. Thousands of others saw him and could care less that he was there. Indeed, some of them beat him and crucified him for messing with their lives. Seeing is not believing. Simeon died at peace not because he saw the Lord but because he loved the Lord, and he loved the Lord long before he came to see him. It was Simeon's love that allowed him to believe and hope even on the days when the Lord was not visibly present, on the days when Simeon was lonely and felt poorly. The glory of Simeon came not from his seeing the Lord one day but in his living bravely through all those days when the Lord seemed occupied somewhere else. So too, Paul saw Jesus once, but he believed every day thereafter. It was because he believed that he was able to face the difficulties of his life. It was his believing and not his seeing that enabled him to say: "We never become discouraged. Even though our physical being is gradually decaying, yet our spiritual being is renewed day after day. . . . What can be seen lasts only for a time, but what cannot be seen lasts forever" (2 Cor 4:16, 18 *Good News Bible*). It was because of his belief and not because of his vision that Paul was able to say: "We know that God, who raised the Lord Jesus to life, will also raise us up with Jesus and bring us, together with you, into his presence" (2 Cor 4:14 *GNB*).

When I grew out of childhood, my parents stopped coming to me every night before I slept. They helped me grow by forcing me to put away the things of a child. I learned to sleep peacefully even without the constant affirmation that I would wake again. I came to recognize the sounds of love close by in my evening darkness. I learned how to pray alone. Like Simeon and Paul I waited in hope for the day described in Hosea:

He will heal us. . . . He will revive us after two days;
On the third day he will raise us up, to live in his presence . . .
as certain as the dawn is his coming, . . .
He will come to us like the rain, like the spring rain that waters the earth (Hos 6:1-6).

Fourth Sunday: Blindness

God wants no human being to be blind, but many of us are through much of our lives. We are deep in the forest of our own needs, and we cannot see our God for the trees. Our surface wants take up our attention, and we cannot see beyond them. We are thus blind to much of the reality of life.

Of course in the beginning we were physically blind to everything. In the womb we could not see, because there was no light. We did not mind. We were more concerned with our growing life than with outside events. But later this changed. We were pulled from the womb into light. We were smacked at one end, and our eyes popped open at the other. We looked around and uttered our first cry; there were so many things to desire! We did not know what they were, but they seemed pretty and interesting, and we wanted them for ourselves. We saw the surface of things and said, "That is all there is!" Babies are the ultimate empiricists.

The trouble with living a whole life on the surface of things is that we cannot see more important realities. Living on the surface of life prevents us from appreciating the depths in others and in ourselves. Of course if everyone around us is a "surface" person, we will never learn what we are missing. Living in a kingdom of the blind, we will never know that we are blind.

Even under the best of conditions, a certain amount of blindness in life can be expected. We are like the man born physically blind in the Gospel story (John 9: 1-41). Our sometime blindness is part of the human condition after Adam. We are told that it was not always so. At one time humans walked with and talked to the Lord. But for some unknown reason this was not enough. Humans looked elsewhere. Adam turned his eyes away from God, and when he looked back, God was gone. Adam thereby learned a great truth about God. God is something like a reflection in a mirror. He disappears when we do not care to look. He disappears when we look but will only accept a reflection of our own desires. Adam learned the great truth about human seeing: we must *want* to see before blindness can be cured.

The story of the blind man told in John 9 brings out the same truth. If he had not cried out for Jesus, he would have died blind. Perhaps he lived for many years without even thinking about being cured. He did tell the Pharisees that no one had ever been cured before. Perhaps in his previous life of blindness he was dominated by the principle of those afraid to dream: "Miracles do not happen. Nothing can ever happen for the first time." Perhaps he was afraid that if he took a chance on something new, he would lose what he had. He was afraid that if he made a fuss about being cured, the passersby would not give him the alms to support his blindness. It is not unknown that a human chooses making a living over seeing the truth.

The blind man was cured because he was willing to risk all for a chance at seeing. He wanted to see above all, and he was perfectly willing to do an apparently useless thing—washing in an ordinary pool—upon the instructions of a stranger. It took him a long time to find Jesus, but this was not because he did not *want* Jesus. He just could not see that he was in the neighborhood. It is quite different for those of us raised in the Christian faith. We know Jesus is around. If we cannot see him, it is because we are too distracted to look. We are blind but not because we see too little. We are blind because we look too much. We go through life looking here and there, there and here, like bees flitting from one blossom to another. We sip the sweet nectar of the present till boredom prompts us to fly on to the next adventure. We are not attuned to sitting still and looking for the sweet God within us. We see everything outside and nothing inside. We are blind to the presence of God lying just below the surface of things.

Our blindness is not always cured swiftly. St. Augustine rummaged around the surface of life for thirty years before he dove to the depths. He searched every nook and cranny of his surface world for the meaning of his life but did not find the answer until he closed his eyes and looked deep inside his own being. There below the surface of himself he found his Lord and understood that it had been the Lord deep inside that had driven him to search. The Lord had been there all the time, but St. Augustine found him only when he had closed his eyes to earthly ambition, sensual lust, and selfishness.

Years later, St. Augustine was still rejoicing over his cure. He told his friends:

What a great gift is given to a blind man when the doctor comes and cures his blindness! To finally *see* the light! A man cured of blindness can find no adequate gift to return to his healer. What is equal to the gift of sight restored? The cured blind man may give his healer gold piled upon gold but his healer gave *him* light. If you ever wished to remind the newly seeing man that in giving gold he truly gave nothing, just put him in a room without light and tell him to look for the colors of all his gold! What then shall we give to that doctor who healed our earthly eyes so that we might see the colors of eternity? (*2nd Commentary on Psalm 36:8*).

When St. Augustine was cured of his blindness, he gave his Savior his life. We who are still blind must be prepared to do the same. Indeed, such readiness for a cure is the beginning of the cure.

Monday of the Fourth Week: Death at an Early Age

The good may indeed die young, but the young do not always die well. And when the young die, we seldom or ever take it well. Even when they make their rush to resurrection peacefully (like the fetus sleeping into eternity without ever experiencing the pains and pleasures of conscious life), we are left with the conviction that something terrible has happened. We say, "How sad it is that one so young should die so soon!" and then we lapse into silence. The death of the young is not to be explained, only endured. There is always a deep sorrow left behind for those who must continue the trek to resurrection alone.

The paradox is that we feel much the same way when one we love seems to outlive life, continuing to live and breathe well beyond the time of functioning with dignity and pride. If it is sad to see someone die who has never known too much life, so too is it sad to see someone live who has pleaded with the Lord for blessed relief in death. The three tragedies of this life are that some do not live long enough, some live too long, and the rest of us do not do very well in the life that is given. It is not a rotten world, but it certainly is mixed up.

God knows it is mixed up and is not happy about it. He is not indifferent to human suffering. He wants to make things better. Thus he promised Isaiah:

> Lo, I am about to create new heavens and a new earth . . .
> No longer shall there be in it an infant who lives but a few days, or an old man who does not round out his full lifetime (Isa 65:17-20).

Jesus almost always did something for the young who were terribly sick or who had already rushed through death at an early age. He cured the son of the royal official (John 4:43-54). He brought back to life the son of the widow of Naim (Luke 7:18-23) and the daughter of Jairus (Mark 5:21-43). Perhaps Jesus was driven by the memory of the Holy Innocents, those babies who had died because of him. In any case it is clear that he did not like a world in which children die young. He did not cure all of them in his own day. He certainly does not do so today. But of these young sufferers, especially, the prophecy of Isaiah is true: "He himself takes up their infirmities and bears the burden of their ills" (Isa 53:4). This is not the world that Jesus-God wanted, and he cannot change it that much just now. But he could endure it, and this he did for thirty years or so, the time allowed to him by the hatred of his human foes.

He endured the loss of loved ones. He watched the young die too soon and the old linger beyond comfortable days. He cured some little children who were very sick and sadly watched others die. In life and death he called them to him, saying: "Let the little children come to me, and do not hinder them, for of such is the kingdom of God" (Mark 10:14). In their life and after their death the scene depicted by Mark takes place: "He put his arms around them and laying his hands upon them he began to bless them" (Mark 10:16*).

We who are still trapped in this incomplete life must still endure the death of the young and the suffering of the old. We must make the best of things. We can at least be happy that our dead children are beyond suffering. We can pray to them to help us get over missing them so much. And for our suffering elderly, we at least can embrace them in their suffering. We may not be able to take away their pain, but we can make sure that they are not alone as they wait for the coming of the Lord.

And as we endure, we can remind ourselves of the promise made to the human race by God: Lo, I am about to create new heavens and a new earth. The things of the past shall not be remembered or come to mind. Instead, there shall always be rejoicing and happiness in what I create (Isa 65:17-21).

---

*This passage and the previous one cited are from *The New Testament of Our Lord and Savior Jesus Christ*—revision of the Challoner-Rheims Version by the Confraternity of Christian Doctrine.

Tuesday of the Fourth Week: Feeling Poorly

For most of us still on the road to resurrection, the day will
come when we will begin to fall apart. We will have reached our
days for feeling poorly, and the running will become hard. It is hard
to worry about your future when you have pain in the here and
now. Illness takes up all your attention. Days are filled with going
to doctors (or waiting for them to come to you), taking pills, and
recording each new symptom for posterity. When you are very sick,
you spend much time listening to your body and little time listening to noises beyond your illness. When you are very sick, it is hard
to think of anything beyond the fact that "I am very sick."

When illness continues for a long time or when you realize that
it is indeed the preamble to your death, you make your own addi-
tions to the sentiments of Paul in Galatians (2:19-20):

I have been crucified with Christ (in this my terrible illness),
and the life I live now is not my own (This dying life cannot be *my* life!
My life is a life of vitality, not of
such deadly weakness!);

I still live my human life, but it is a life of faith in the Son of God who
loved me and gave himself for me (I live now only because of hope,
hope that tomorrow it will be
better).

It takes strength to live through days of serious illness gracefully. It takes *heroic* strength when the illness is prolonged and we
are alone with it. It is because of this truth that the story of Jesus'
cure of the man sick for thirty-eight years is so satisfying (John
5:1-16). The poor man's illness was made even more terrible because
it was so unnecessary. For thirty-eight years the poor man could
see the means of a cure right at his feet, but he was unable to reach
out and grasp it. To be cured, he needed only to be the first one
into the waters of Siloam after the healing angel touched its surface. For thirty-eight years he never made it in time. For thirty-eight

years people stepped over him and around him (and probably sometimes upon him), rushing into the waters before him. For thirty-eight years humans had seen him lying on the banks of the pool and did not care. Jesus saw him only once and immediately cured him. The story is very satisfying.

What is not satisfying is the fact that God does not cure more of us of the terrible diseases of this life. Over the years I have sat with many folks with killing diseases. I have prayed for them and with them. I have given them the sacrament of the sick. I have given them the sacrament of reconciliation. I have given them the Body and Blood of the Lord. I gave them all these good things, and then they died. They died at peace, but they died. They did not recover. The Lord was close to them, but these he did not cure. The experience has convinced me that I had best learn how to live with feeling poorly because some day the "feeling poorly" will not be cured except by death. I may continue to hope for a cure from the Lord, but I must not expect it. I must learn to live with my illnesses and to learn from them and to find in them the special graces of endurance that I need.

To be sick is never a good thing (and it is a blasphemy to say that the Lord is happy when humans are sick), but some good can be derived from it. The very sick can accomplish much of value to themselves and to others. They can, for example, gracefully allow themselves to be cared for. In so doing they can lessen the pain of those who love them and give to those caring folks an opportunity for grace. When we take care of another, we are forced to break out of the natural selfishness that infects us all. Our lives expand when we care for someone who is helpless. The very sick can, as they approach death, help those watching come closer to God.

The very sick can perfect themselves by humbly accepting the care of others. Being cared for in a terminal illness completes the cycle of life. When we were young, we all had to be cared for, but we were not conscious of the need and hence got no merit for accepting it. When we are very ill or very old, we must consciously say "yes" to our weakness and submit to the care of others. After a life of being in charge of life, such acceptance can be therapeutic if done in the right spirit. If we have spent our days of vigor in caring for others, valuing our independence, coming and going as we please, we can develop a delusion of omnipotence. We can become convinced that we are God almighty, or at least God's gift to humankind. It is hard to maintain that delusion when we are too weak to get out of bed unaided and too addled to control our natural functions.

Being cared for can remind us that at the very root of our lives we are incompetent. We cannot add a moment to the times of our lives. We cannot insure that the quality of life will always be good. We forget such things when we are having a good time. When we are having the time of our life, we forget that each moment of our time hangs by a thread. All this changes when we are very sick. Each moment becomes tentative. We are reminded that for us to live at all we must have the cooperation of powers beyond our control:

the good pleasure of the tides,
the caprice of the earth's molten core,
the passions of the winds,
the graces and providence of the Lord.

When we feel good, we sometimes act as though we were infinite. When we feel bad, we hope that we are immortal.

Just now I feel pretty good (and thus I can write about feeling bad), but when my days of illness come I hope I can make my own the brave words of Paul:

But to keep me from being puffed up with pride because of the many wonderful things I saw, I was given a painful physical ailment, which acts as Satan's messenger to beat me and keep me from being proud. Three times I prayed to the Lord about this and asked him to take it away. But his answer was: "My grace is all you need, for my power is strongest when you are weak." I am most happy, then, to be proud of my weaknesses, in order to feel the protection of Christ's power over me. I am content with weaknesses, insults, hardships, persecutions, and difficulties for Christ's sake. For when I am weak, then I am strong (2 Cor 12:7-10, *GNB*).

Perhaps Paul was saved as much by his days of patient enduring as by his days of brave preaching. Perhaps the same will be true of me and of you. As our bodies weaken, our spirit strength will be proven. I hope we pass the test. I hope we take our medicine. I hope we know that the Lord is with us in our last illness as he is during every day of our lives.

Wednesday of the Fourth Week: "I Will Never Forget You"

We are coming to the end of our times. This is what the Lord tells us. He tells us this through the words of Scripture. He tells us this through the descending spiral of our strength. He repeats his message again and again, because he is a realist and would not lie. But along with this somber truth he tries to teach us how to live with the truth, with the truth of living in a world where disaster is ever near. He teaches us how to live in a world where every individual's life hangs by a thread, those fragile arterial connections in our brain and heart which could explode without warning. We live at this moment at the pleasure of temporarily dormant killing germs. We are as alive today and will be alive tomorrow because of the luck of not being in the wrong place at the wrong time.

Our human civilization ("the glory of humanity" we call it when we are being pompous) has a fragile existence. We relish our sophisticated pleasures, but we play them out in the midst of madness. St. Augustine's remark about the fifth century is no less true today: "Not only along the frontiers but throughout all the provinces we owe our peace to the sworn oaths of the barbarians." (*Letter* 47:2) And on those days when it seems that the whole world will erupt in nuclear war, we fear that the prophecy of Malachi will at last be fulfilled: "Lo, the day is coming, blazing like an oven, when all the proud and all evildoers will be stubble, and the day that is coming will set them on fire, leaving them neither root nor branch" (Mal 3:19-20).

This is part of the real world in which we must live out our days. This is the world in which we must someday face our death. Faced with this I ask the Lord: "How can I live until I die? How can I die in peace?" And the Lord answers: "You shall not be lost. Your endurance will win you your life" (see Luke 21:18-19). I ask the Lord: "How can I live in this troublesome world?" He answers: "By enduring." I ask: "But how can I endure?" He answers: "By love."

He is saying to me and you that even in the midst of turmoil we can care for each other. We can do our best not to hurt each other. We can take responsibility for the pieces of life that we control and do our best to have them dominated by love. If we live in a democratic state, we can take responsibility for our leaders. If we live in a family, we can try to be instruments of peace rather than aggravations. If we are involved in doing business, we can make sure that our business dealing is fair. It just does not make good sense to do otherwise in a world that can end for us at any moment. There are no lasting monuments except the pleasant memories we leave with others. There is no success except the success of being embraced forever by those who love us.

We can get through this life if we know that somebody cares that we exist. It is hard to live alone in a crowded, rushing world. And yet sometimes that is our destiny. St. Augustine himself felt the special burden of old age that comes with the realization that all your loves have died before you. If such times come to us, we must try to remember that we have a friend who will never leave us. It is the friend who speaks to each one of us individually through the words of Isaiah:

> "Can a woman forget her own baby
>   and not love the child she bore?
> Even if a mother should forget her child,
>   I will never forget you.
>   . . . I can never forget you!
>   I have written your name on the palms of my hands" (49:15-16 *GNB*).

Thursday of the Fourth Week: Middle-aged Madness

The middle years of my life seem to be times either for growing a little wise or growing a little crazy. The pendulum swings from one extreme to the other depending on the mood of the moment. Whether a particular day is to be sapient or sappy depends on whether I accept the time of my life or just try to have the time of my life. The wisdom of middle age is to realize that I am no longer a kid but that I am not yet dead. I can no longer be young in body, but there is no reason why I cannot be young at heart. The move from cute to svelte to saggy is irreversible, but there is no need to get depressed. There is always something left behind when the bloom of youth vanishes. And even though the remaining "me" is just an old pot, there is no reason why I cannot be filled up again with vibrant experiences suited to my mature life.

It takes a few years to develop wisdom. Growing up in Philadelphia, my early goal was simple survival. I could not put my life in perspective because I had but few years under my belt. Unfortunately, as the years lengthen and the belt tightens about increasing girth, a panic can arise. One begins to realize that one has passed one's physical prime. The days of swinging and jiving down life's highways are over. The rest of the trip must be made by bus. The values of one's youth seem only half-accomplished and forever irretrievable. One is tempted to follow the example of the ancient Israelites in the desert and cast everything aside, make a molten calf and cry: "This is my God!" (see Exod 32).

When the temptation to such middle-aged madness strikes, it is important for me to realize that it is not a sign (necessarily) that I am sick. It means only that I am growing up. Midlife fear at the prospect of ebbing life is characteristic of any human who desperately wants to live and who wants to live well. We have a thirst to live forever, and when it seems that our life is slipping away, when it seems that our great ambition for worldly success will never be accomplished, when it seems certain that we shall never be able to possess love without some future separation, panic sets in, and we begin to scramble around looking for some new beginning.

The tendency is as old as the human race. Perhaps a touch of this madness infected Adam and Eve when they became bored with Eden and looked around for some place better. Even the book of Wisdom contains a description of this middle-aged malaise:

> Undisciplined souls, they have gone astray. They imagined that they had nations in their power, but they themselves lay prisoners of the dark . . . They were terrified by apparitions . . . Those who professed to drive out fears and disorders from sick souls, themselves fell sick of a ridiculous terror . . . Even when there was nothing frightful to scare them . . . they died convulsed in fright . . . Wickedness is confessedly very cowardly, and it condemns itself. Under pressure from conscience it always assumes the worst. Fear, indeed, is nothing other than the abandonment of the supports offered by reason. The less you rely within yourself on these, the more alarming it is not to know the cause of your suffering . . . They stayed clamped to the spot in this prison without bars . . . The whole world was shining with brilliant light and unhindered went on with its work. Over them alone there spread a heavy darkness. But heavier than any darkness was the burden they were to themselves (see Wis 17:1-20).

Now in my middle years I must not become so paralyzed. I must stop mooning about my past and look to my future. I can still be young in spirit. I can still look to eternal life with childlike wonder. God loves me at any age. If he is here, then the promise of Proverbs will always be true for me: "If you sit down, you will not be afraid. When you lie down, your sleep will be sweet" (see Prov 3:24).

Friday of the Fourth Week: The April Fool

It is fitting that the Lenten season, the season that commemorates the days of our lives, usually includes the first days of April. That means we can celebrate the special feast dedicated to me and you: April Fool's Day. We hope and pray that someday we will be included in that great November feast of All Saints, but that is not certain for us yet. The invitations have gone out, but it is not yet certain that we will finally and forever accept and go to God's party. But most of us have already qualified to be April Fools. Most of us have already been tricked into believing that we are more than we are or have been tricked into believing that we are less than God's love has made us.

I have a fond memory of past April Fool's days. The feast has a special meaning for me. It was the day on which I passed my doctoral exam in philosophy. ("April Fool, Plato!") Moreover, I was born in April. ("April Fool, Mom and Dad!") April Fool's Day was a great day in West Philadelphia when I was growing up. In the last days of March, our neighborhood gang of ruffians would get together and make our own the words of the book of Wisdom:

> Let us beset the just one, because he is obnoxious to us;
> he sets himself against our doings . . .
> merely to see him is a hardship for us, Because his life is not like other men's, and different are his ways (Wis 2:12-15).

Inspired by such sentiments, we would declare war on all fools, that is, anybody who was not exactly like us. We would trick them as best we could and then run away shouting, "April Fool! April Fool!" Looking back, I can see that it was a silly exercise because the greatest fools were ourselves, living as though *this day* was forever and pretending that we were not rushing to resurrection. But I guess we were no worse than the rest of the human race. Our April Fool games are just tiny symbols of the tricks that were played on Jesus-God when he walked the paths of this earthly life. The list of tricks played on him is quite long and quite cruel:

> The innkeeper said: "There is no room for you in the inn." ("April Fool, Jesus!")
> Herod said: "Tell me where the baby is so that I can go and worship him." ("April Fool, Jesus!")
> The lepers said: "We believe in you, Jesus. Only cure us and we shall be eternally thankful." ("April Fool, Jesus!")

The leaders of the people said; "Don't be afraid. we will never bring
harm to you. "("April Fool, Jesus!")

The disciples said: "We will go with you to Jerusalem and die with you."
("April Fool, Jesus!")

And the people of Jerusalem said: "Hail Jesus!" and Pilate said: "I am
here to insure justice!" and Peter said: "I will never deny you!" and the
crowd said: "We want Barrabas!" and the soldier said: "You can carry
the cross. It's not heavy!" and they gave him a vinegar-soaked sponge
saying: "Here is some sweet water, Jesus!" ("April Fool, Jesus!")

But then came Jesus' turn. Then Jesus began to play his great
good tricks on the human race. And thus it was that on Easter Morn
ing Jesus said to Mary: "Here I am, Mary. April fool!" And soon
after he said to his disciples: "Here, feel my wounds! I have risen
from the dead! April fool!" And later he said to his first priests
"Go and forgive sins! No human need be damned! April fool, sin
ners!" And then as he left this world he looked at all of us and said
"I will never leave you alone! April fool, humanity!"

If a trick is an unexpected event, it is not disrespectful to say
that Easter was God's second great trick on the human race. Crea
tion was his first trick. It was simply beyond imagining that some
thing should exist where before there had been nothing. But perhaps
Easter was even greater. After the human rejection of God (nothing
rejecting everything), it was beyond belief that God would still care
about his recalcitrant creatures. And that he should actually love
them and die for them so that they could live forever with him was
just too much to hope for!

But who knows? Perhaps the greatest surprise of all will come
when we die. Paul for one says that we cannot even *dream* of the
good things God has prepared for us on the other side of death
We will close our eyes in the sleep of death and then suddenly wake
up in the arms of the Lord. We will hear him laugh and say, "April
fool, my love!"

Saturday of the Fourth Week: Turning the Corner

It was the beginning of Jesus' last fortnight. In two weeks he would be in his grave. Even now he could hear the whisper of the forces that would destroy him: "Let us destroy the tree in its vigor; let us cut him off from the land of the living" (Jer 11:19). He was only thirty some years old, but the time had come for him (as it will come for all of us) to turn that last corner in life and begin his last plummeting downhill run towards resurrection.

The road to resurrection is without turns only for the very young, those who die in the womb or soon after. For the rest of us, life is more complex. Looking back, I see my life more like a maze than a desert highway plunging straight and true towards the distant cool mountains. I always seem to be turning corners, facing surprising futures. I am ever coming upon new adventures for which I am unprepared. I keep turning corners in my life, finding exotic new vistas.

The most radical change in my life up till now was the moment when I began to be. There was little conscious impact at the moment. There was no "me" before the event and precious little "me" after. Even now the words, "once I was nothing and then I was someone," seem limp instruments for recording the amazing way in which I began to be. My birth was the next corner turned. I leaped from the quiet confinement of my mother's womb and for the first time was on my own. The next great shock, the next new corner turned, was when I first fell in love. When I first found someone who meant more to me than myself, I moved from "being on my own" to "being unable to live without another." Nothing in my previous experience could prepare me for turning that corner and finding love. Nothing in my past came close to imitating it. Nothing in my future can substitute for it. Once in love, I pray that no future corner turned will rob me of that love.

There will be other corners turned in my life. That is certain. There is the gradual corner-turning that comes in simply growing older. There was a day when I woke up and realized that the days

left to me on this earth were probably less than the days already
spent. My future was shorter than my past. Such a realization
prompts a change in attitude towards your life. The good things
become more precious. You are more impatient with those who
would waste your time. You try to prepare to "let go" of things
that seemed so important in your days of youth. You try to develop
a freedom so that you will be able to turn that last corner in life
without entanglement. That last corner is the day when we know
we are facing our death.

Turning any of these corners takes courage. In each case we come
face-to-face with the new, with the unaccustomed, and we may be
afraid that we are unable to deal with it. We may become so attached to our present that we are unwilling to give it up in favor
of an uncertain future. When faced with first love we may say: "I
cannot be bound by love just yet; I am not ready to give up my
freedom." When faced with aging we may cry: "I cannot be growing old! I have too many young things left to do! I have not had
enough springtime dancing; I am not ready for my autumn years."
When faced with the fact of our death we may say: "I cannot be
coming to the end of my life! There are too many things left to do!
I am needed; I am wanted. It cannot be that I soon must die!" Whether there is the promise of good or bad, turning a corner is a terribly new experience, and we may be very much afraid.

It is truly sad if this is the case for us, because we must turn
corners whether we want to or not. And there can be exhilaration
in change if it is done in the right spirit. Having gone through the
change we frequently find that the new experience is much better
than the old. Who, once born, fights to return to the womb? Who,
once in love, would wish that it were any other way? And with
regard to growing old, at least one old man (St. Augustine) said
that he would rather die than go back to growing up.

Perhaps the realization that past corners turned brought joy will
help me face that final turning which is my death. I will say to
myself: "Well, I have turned a lot of corners in my life and survived. I have survived being born. I have survived growing old.
I have survived falling in love. I have survived being separated from

my love. I have survived all the twists and turns of living; perhaps I will survive my dying. Jesus promises that it will be so. He promises that this last great event will not be all that terribly bad and that a great good awaits me just around the corner."

With a hopeful attitude I can make my last steps towards resurrection as fruitful as my first. Like Jesus in his last fortnight of life, I will rush bravely to face my death, wishing perhaps that things were different but not despairing because they are not. There is no reason why my last days cannot be filled with new graces for myself and for others. With the help of God, I will turn that last corner putting the finishing touches on a life honestly lived. Perhaps I will hear those words of the Lord directed towards every human in the midst of life-shaking change: "Do not be afraid. Every hair of your head has been counted" (see Matt 10:30-31).

Fifth Sunday: Losing a Love

We are told that Jesus loved Lazarus, but that seemed to be no help. Lazarus died anyway. Even having God as a friend does not slow a man's rush to resurrection. Nor does the friendship of God take away the ache in the hearts of those left behind. Martha and Mary wept at the loss of their brother. Jesus did not stop their tears. He stood beside them and wept too (John 11:31-35). Having God as a friend does not stop us weeping when we lose a love. It may, however, help us get through.

In thinking about my absent loves and aching for them, I am consoled by knowing that there is nothing wrong with me. It is not a sign that I am selfish. It is not a sign that God is not with me. It is only a sign that I am a human who is very much in love even though my love has gone. I am not silly when I weep. I am not being churlish in not following the advice, "Cheer Up!" as in these phrases:

"I know you have just lost your baby, but Cheer Up!"
"I know you have lost your spouse, but Have a nice day!"
"I know you have lost your love, but Smile! The Lord loves you!"

Even Jesus-God could not smile when he lost a loved one so I should not be guilty when I must weep for absent loves, at least for a while.

It is natural to be in pain, because when I lose my love I lose a piece of me. I lose one who was inside me, who knew those inner parts of me that no stranger ever sees: my secret fears and passions, my hopes, my childish confusions. All of us have our public facades, those presentations of ourselves that others expect of us. It is not a deception because our public side is a true aspect of our person. But it is only a partial picture, and it is sometimes distorted by our puffing up this or that attractive aspect of ourselves (our gentleness or exuberance or dignity or whatever) demanded by the moment. Our public side may thus make loud noises in favor of positions only lightly held. We are so loving to our new loves that they may not know of the hard core of selfishness that lurks just below the surface. It takes an old love to see that core. It takes a good old love to keep loving us despite that corrupt core. Sometimes, too, we are scared to death at the very moment that we play hero to our kids. We play the saint to those who come to us for a prayer or an answer to life's mystery, and never hint to them that deep down inside we are not too well tied together. If we become adept at these roles, we may even come to believe that we are indeed lovely and brave and holy. We should know better if we looked seriously at ourselves. We are deep mysteries even to ourselves, but sometimes we can get an inkling of our dark sides in the dreams and fantasies that occupy our unguarded moments. Some of them point to our violent side, our rapacious side, our scared side. They show that we are not all sweetness and light. They point out that we are human after all. It is a therapeutic revelation if we accept it. If darkness is a fact, it is better confronted than ignored. But often we try to ignore it, because we are afraid that no one will like us if they know we are not perfect.

A true love is one who loves us despite our scars. A true love is one to whom we can reveal our secret selves without fear of being rejected. A true love is one before whom we can stand naked without fear of laughter or horror. We have a great gift when we find such a love. And when we lose such love, it is a terrible, terrible loss. When my love leaves me it is another door slamming shut, imprisoning me in myself. When such a love leaves me, I feel that I am suffocating in my own moldiness, the decay that comes from a life too long closed in upon itself.

When I lose a love, I probably should say, "Remember that the Lord knows you and loves you!" Perhaps I should say that, but it will not make me feel any better. Just now, as I live out my days in this life, I need my God *and* my human loves. Maybe that is why Jesus told me to love both. He knew that we needed both. He knew that having one does not make us feel better about losing the other. He does not want us to ever sacrifice his love for the love of a human being. Nor is it likely that he will ever demand of us that we sacrifice a love for his sake. The scene of Abraham and Isaac is remembered precisely because it is so extraordinary. In most cases God is very happy when we have our human loves, and he weeps with us, as he did with Martha and Mary, when we lose them.

He promises that someday the weeping will end. Someday he will bring all our loves back to us, as he once brought Lazarus back to his sisters. When that day comes, everybody will be very happy but happiest of all will be that God who once stood by the grave of a human being and wept for the loss of one whom he loved.

Monday of the Fifth Week: The Passion of the Old

The story of Susanna in Daniel 13 is a harsh, violent story (so violent indeed that the Church makes its use in the Mass optional). Sadly it reflects violence that is not unknown in human history. Its warning is clear. As long as a person is alive, there is the chance that they will sacrifice eternity for a moment of passion, whether it be a moment of sensual satisfaction, a moment of revenge, a moment of pride, or a moment of anger. We are always liable to the temptation to put all our eggs into the basket of this moment, to sacrifice everything for this instant's satisfaction.

The story also warns that age is no protection from such passion. It says that the old can sometimes do terrible damage to the innocent. It says: "There is no fool like an old fool and an old fool is often a cruel fool." The old men in the story were as much creatures of anger as of desire. They seemed to hate Susanna because she was everything that they were not, young, lovable, pious. Their passion was to destroy her, not possess her. They acted on their nurtured fantasies and came close to such destruction, but in the end destroyed only themselves.

So many of the terrible things we do begin as nurtured fantasy. We dream about things being different. We dream about being lords of the universe, about being better than anybody else. We fantasize that we have been unjustly injured by fate. We fantasize that someday we can possess this one or that one. When the young fantasize about the future, it is not particularly dangerous. When we are young, we dream about what could be. Such innocent dreams are akin to hope and do no damage. But when we are old, our dreams are sometimes about what might have been, and these can be dangerous. They can lead to a burning anger that our past was not indeed different. They can lead to present passionate pretending that things *are* different. They can lead to a terrible waste of time. Dreaming about what might have been can prevent living what is.

This is not to deny that there can be radical change in the life of the elderly. Sometimes it happens. Sometimes one finds new loves in the autumn of life. It is possible to start a new career at any age. But radical changes after a certain point in life are at least unusual. Now, in the midst of my life, I find myself in a particular place. I am here very probably because it is the best place for me to be. I am formed by my history and my powers to be the man doing what I am doing. In my middle fifties I do not have the time or the finances to become a brain surgeon. My clumsy hands and dreaming mind are better fitted to being a philosopher anyway. In my middle fifties I do not have the energy to be a "swinger." My loves are set now, and they are stuck with me. Hopefully I am set with my God too. I am not likely to find a new God who will make me believe in him/her. I am not likely to be called to strange new heavens nor be threatened with some new hell. What I will be is much like what I am. And what I am (not what I imagine myself to be) is what will be saved or lost.

Jesus understands why we humans dream our dreams and sometimes lose ourselves in moments of passion. Thus he did not condemn the poor human taken in adultery (John 8:1-11). His only demand was, "Go and sin no more!" He understood that we humans sometimes go a little crazy. He understood that there is something missing in our lives and that sometimes we reach out in passion and try to grab at anything that seems to satisfy our hunger. Jesus understands us and forgives us, but he cannot take away the hurt caused by our passions. He cannot give back the precious time wasted in chasing our fantasies.

As my years lengthen, I am well advised to recognize that there will always be something missing in my life this side of resurrection. There is thus no use in wishing that things were different. I must focus on the reality of my life and get on with doing those things that my years have proven I can do well.

Tuesday of the Fifth Week: "Are We There Yet?"

Faith tells us that in our last days we are not waiting for death. We are waiting for the Lord. Of course this was not exactly true for Jesus during his last two weeks of life. He was not waiting for the Lord. He *was* the Lord. But even he must have spent some time in anxious anticipation, waiting for the suffering to be over, waiting to get on with the good things after death. Like any human, Jesus-God must have been a bit impatient waiting for things to happen. I would not be surprised if on that first long excursion he made into Egypt, he kept asking Joseph, "Are we there yet?" And at the end of his life the meaning of his great cry to his Father, "Let this chalice pass!" could very well have been, "Let's get over with it, Father. Let's get on with the dying so that I can go home!"

We humans spend most of our lives waiting for something to happen. I remember my seashore trips when I was a child. I cried most of the way. I didn't know where I was going but was anxious to get there. I would cry, "Are we there yet?" even before we were out of the garage. Like any father, Dad did not beat me into silence. He would give me a Philadelphia pretzel to suck on (the time was B.D.—before dentures), and this would keep me happy for a while. But by midtrip I would become restless. I gummed my soggy pretzel and made my own the words of the Israelites wandering through the wastelands: "Why have you brought us up from Egypt to die in this desert, where there is no food or water? We are disgusted with this wretched food" (Num 21:5). And then I would renew my wail, "Are we there yet?" Usually by the end of the trip, my whining body had been relegated to the rumble seat, while Mom and Dad sat inside protected by tightly closed windows. They would not "put down" their youngest, but they saw no reason to "put up" with him.

Hopefully God is more patient with our caterwauling. He realizes that we are all waiting for the Lord in different ways and are anxious to get the tiresome waiting finished. We all must wait, but we wait in different fashion. Many waited for Jesus during his earthly life, and their differences are symbols of the different ways in which we sometimes wait for the Lord. Mary, for example, waited to see the Jesus hidden deep inside her. Hers was a truly joyful waiting. She could not see Jesus yet, but she was so close to him that she could *feel* his presence in her life. She did not see him, but neither did she need to believe in him. She *knew* that he was with her, even though he was still hidden from her sight.

John the Baptist waited to see the Lord in a desert. Outwardly John's life was barren, but he believed in the coming of Jesus, and he was able to dance for joy despite his desert life. But John was a bit confused in his belief. There is a hint that he expected the Lord to come as a conquering hero or as some sort of stern judge. Thus John preached a message of repentance. He cried: "Be on guard! The king is coming to settle accounts!" He must have been very surprised when the Lord finally came to him. He had expected to kneel before a king. He never expected to end up baptizing a carpenter.

The Magi, those wise men from the East, waited to see a Lord they could only hope for. They had no clear knowledge of where or how or when the Lord would come to this earth. They began their journey believing only in the star. But they had hope, and it was this hope that drove them to visit a land that they did not know to find a Lord who was beyond their wildest dreams.

Mary and John and the Magi waited for the same saving Lord but in quite different ways. And so too do we. Some of us, like St. Augustine, are destined to find the Lord as the Magi did. We wander through foreign lands through unfamiliar hills and valleys, following faint glimmers of inspiration that encourage us to go on with our search, even though we are not certain where we are going. Just as the young Augustine was driven through the ideologies and passions of his day looking for one to love, so we are sometimes driven through life with only a hope that if we do not give up the search, someday we shall find the Lord of our heart's desire.

Others follow the path of the Baptist in their waiting. They know something of the Lord and they believe in him, but they do not really understand him. They put special demands on him. They say: "If you really loved me, Lord, you would solve all my problems." Especially at the end of life, the waiting can become painful. From prison we cry with the Baptist, "Are you really the Messiah?" We cannot believe that our Savior would not come and save us from our death. We pray in faith, "Come Lord!" and weep when we are *not* cured, when our dying continues. We expect our Savior to come as a healer of our disease. We are surprised when he comes only as a comforter in our dying. We expected a doctor, not a good friend. But when we get over the shock of this unexpected Jesus, this Jesus who is not going to carry us back into this life but only wait for us in the next, then we rush forward to meet him. We are happy in our last moments of waiting for the next life and fall peacefully asleep in death. And after a life of belief, we begin a life of seeing.

For a few select humans the waiting for the Lord will be like that of Mary waiting for the birth of her Son. The Lord is hidden deep within them, but they can feel his presence. The Lord wants this mode of waiting to be for all of us, but only a few achieve it. Most of us are unwilling to pay the price for this great gift. The price is simply to say "Yes" to the Lord unconditionally and forever. Mary paid the price. She said "Yes" once and meant it. And the Lord came and lived in her; it was that simple.

Our waiting for the Lord, in whatever form it takes, can be especially hard when we perceive that we are near the end of the trip. My childish cry, "Are we there yet!" became almost deafening as we came close to the sea. So, too, in the last few weeks of life, the anticipation of what lies ahead can become almost unbearable. When those days come, it is comforting to know that all those who have waited for the Lord or searched for the Lord or hoped for the Lord, all those who have in any way left a door open for him in their lives, will arrive finally at their happy destination. In those last days it is important to remember the encouragement of Scripture: "Do not, then, surrender your confidence; it will have great reward. You need patience to do God's will and receive what he has promised. For just a brief moment, and he who is to come will come; he will not delay" (Heb 10:35-37).

In my last days I hope I can follow the advice of Augustine:

Look ahead to the one who leads you. Don't look back to the places from which he has led you (*Commentary on Psalm 75*:16). Forget about those things that are behind you. Forget about the sins of your past. Reach out towards what lies before you (*Commentary on Psalm 130*:14).
Make sure you stay on the right path. Don't fall off on the left

through despair. Don't fall off on the right through presumption. . . . Run bravely along the right path because it will lead you home (*Commentary on Psalm 183:4*).

Someday, if I do not give up, I will cry to the Lord, "Are we there yet?" and hear his response, "Yes, my love, we are."

Wednesday of the Fifth Week: Freedom Lost—Freedom Gained

Jesus once said the following words to those who believed in him, "If you live according to my teaching . . . the truth will set you free" (John 8:31-32). It is an odd promise. We never seem to be free. And belief in Jesus seems to insure no greater freedom in our living or in our dying. There is little freedom in our dying. Sickness and old age can rob us of the ability to do for ourselves at the very end. Lengthening life seems to imprison us rather than free us.

It is for this reason that the dying are sometimes sad. Freedom is one of our greatest desires as human beings. We spend our childhood trying to get beyond dependence on others. We keep testing our parents to see if we can safely transgress their directions without destruction. We sneak out of the house without permission and then we make it beyond the yard and then finally (wonder of wonders) we cross our first street. We survive and begin to burn our bridges behind us. As we grow, we pride ourselves on being in control of our lives. We huff and puff importantly like a puppy briefly unleashed on a barren beach. We gambol on the sand, snuffling from one new jetsam to another, barking loudly about each new find and proudly patrolling the territory that we pretend to control. Sooner or later we are brought to heel. We discover that we do not have absolute control over life or death. We lose our job or we lose our loved ones or we are struck down by illness.

In one way or another we are leashed in and are led away, tail down and grateful for any scraps that fate provides for our nourishment. Our moment on the open beach was exhilarating, but it could not last. Tides inevitably sweep away our playground, and evening must follow even the most brilliant noon. When our personal evening comes, we often become as dependent on others as we were in infancy. Like Christ in his last hours before death, we will depend on others for water and kind words. And after death we will depend on others to care for our remains.

Where is the freedom promised by Christ? Believers seem to die as dependent as unbelievers. One possible answer is that Jesus spoke about the freedom that awaits the other side of death. Our life just now is not our whole story. It is only an introduction to a beginning. This life is less than one particle of the first letter of the eternal story of our life. And the freedom of Jesus will be achieved when we grow into eternity, when we grow up.

But even in this life faith can bring a sort of freedom. In our last days faith can free us from the strings that bind us to this life. In our last days we will no longer be driven by earthly ambition. "Getting ahead" is unimportant to one who is just trying to stay alive. Past hurts are dulled by the prospect of the new life to come. Possessions no longer possess us when we are too weak to use them. As we approach the end of life in faith and hope, we can realize that someone else must take over our responsibilities, someone else must finish the jobs that we began. Faith can give us the confidence to leave the future of this world to someone else as we prepare for the next world. Now, at the end of this life, our only job is to wait for the Lord who is to come. Faith has cut away all other strings that bind us to this world.

At the end of my days there may be some anxiety. I may worry about whether my life has been good enough to merit the freedom that Christ has promised for the next life. I may worry whether I shall die in a fashion that is pleasing to the Lord. I may cry deep inside: "How can I be sure that I am saved when I cannot even eat or drink or turn over on my own? How can I save myself now? I can't do anything for myself!" Perhaps then I shall hear Jesus saying: "I will help you, Donald. Just as kind friends give you water and food and turn you on your deathbed, so shall I be sure to save you. All you need do is put yourself in my hands." I need not worry about having the strength to reach out and hold Jesus at the end. He will be holding me. And finally and forever I shall be free.

Thursday of the Fifth Week: Celebration of Life

As I run with Jesus through the last days of his life on this earth, the question arises, "What has all this to do with *my* life?" Jesus-God's life is so different from mine that it is hard to see how I can identify my history with his. He has said to me (John 8:51-9) that I will exist forever happily if I am true to his word. He has said that his resurrection is a proof that mine will occur, but how can this be since my life is so different from his? His life is summed up in the words, *I AM!* My life is summed up by the words, *"He doesn't have to be!"* The resurrection of Jesus may be a celebration of life, but how is it a celebration of my life?

No two lives are the same even on the purely human level. Thus when some write about their lives they mention things like the smell of freshly baked bread and the sound of a laughing baby and the thrill of an exciting new idea. But this is not the whole of human living. A human life also includes the smell of a ghetto street and the look of a fifteen-year-old suit of clothes and the dazed expression of the terminally ill. Life has its new discoveries and its exciting ideas, but it also has its days of mental deadness when there seems to be nothing new under the sun. Life sometimes has its exciting success but it also has the boredom of a dead end job.

Very few humans enjoy that pretty pink and white life sold to us in store advertisements. Human life is sometimes humdrum, mediocre, imperfect. As I rush with Jesus-God towards the celebration of his Easter rising, I ask, "How does this have any relation to the life I am living and to the death that I must face?"

An answer comes through looking more carefully at the earthly life that Jesus led and the death he died. Jesus's human life and death were different from ours only in that his life and death were more difficult. The death that Jesus faced was not a death of glory. In many ways it was a silly death considered from a purely earthly viewpoint. He was executed for a crime he did not do by a people who did not understand what was going on. His death did not change anyone's mind. In death as in life, Jesus did not convert anyone who did not want to be converted. Jesus did not force himself on anyone who was not at least looking for some sort of better life.

And even those who were changed by contact with Jesus were changed only gradually. Peter was still Peter after his ordination. The main graces given him were humility and courage, the humility to say "I'm sorry" and the courage to persevere in his calling despite his weaknesses. When Jesus' life touched the lives of the humans of his day, it was not an event heralded by trumpets. He solved few human problems immediately. Mostly he gave the courage to endure the bad days and the insight to enjoy the good days.

Thus the resurrection of Jesus was not a return to a divine life. He never ceased to be God. His resurrection was a return to a human life, glorious indeed, but still bearing the scars of his past suffering. Thus his resurrection does not promise something so extraordinary that it has no relationship to my human life this side of the grave. It does not deny my problems. It does not take them away. My faith in Jesus's resurrection will not change my life into some pink and white unreal existence. My faith does not take away my burdens. It simply promises that someday I shall leave them behind. Like Peter on Easter morning, the day will come when I will look into an empty tomb and see the glory of the Lord.

Friday of the Fifth Week: The Rush to Peace

Jesus has said that my rush to resurrection is a rush to peace. When I die, I will not fall apart; I will be pulled together. I must remember this when the tension of my death, the pulling of my soul away from my body, is upon me. In my last days it may be that my body will try to fight my spirit. My body will say: "I must go now. It is time for me to leave. There is nothing for me here." My body will yearn for rest, but my spirit may be unwilling to let go. It may be afraid to leave its accustomed place (this musty old body), because it is afraid that its new place will not be as pleasant. My spirit may be reluctant to leave its loved one alone. My spirit may grasp frantically at this life, because it believes that it has some importance here. It hesitates to move to some new life where all the status of earthly success must be left behind. For whatever reason, it can happen that my spirit and my body will be at war with each other at the very end. I must stop that warring if I am ever to die in peace. I must remind myself that the peace that Jesus promises is not here but hereafter.

God knows that peace is hard to come by in this life. The parts of my being do not fit together nicely. I am wounded and there are disturbances in my body. There are conflicts between body and spirit, between my desires and my reality, between what I want and what I should want. These inner conflicts make me impossible to get along with. How can I be friends with others when I am at war with myself? I war with others to achieve peace, but (as St. Augustine notes) the peace I wish for is always *my* peace. Peace is in having what I want. I try to control others to bring about this peace, because my woundedness prevents me from trusting them. I cannot trust them, because I believe that they have the same weaknesses that prevent me from trusting myself. I am at war with myself and consequently am at war with everyone else.

Jesus says to me that on the other side of death all these wars will end. St. Augustine tells me why this will be so:

In heaven all the good things that God has given us as human beings will reach the peak of their goodness and will stay that way
forever. In heaven every wound suffered in spirit will be healed by
unending wisdom and every illness of body will be overpowered
by resurrection. In heaven our good urges will have free reign. We
shall no longer be at war with our passions. Our "wanting" to do
good will always be effective. We shall once and forever enjoy un-
disturbed rest and unending rest (*City of God* 19:10).

What Augustine is saying is that the rest of heaven will not be caused
by the absence of life but by the absence of conflict. I shall be at
peace with myself not because nothing is working any more but
because everything is working as it should.

Indeed, the peace that is coming is not the calm of silence but
the calm of hearing a delicate melody well-played. When we finally finish our rush to resurrection, we shall have peace not because
we are dead but because we are truly alive for the first time. We
are alive with no ulcer, no gas, no tension headaches. Everything
will work just fine inside us, and outside us we will find only love.
No longer will we fear ending up alone, because we will have ended
up with Jesus. Never again will we search for someone to have fun
with, because we shall play like a child before the throne of the
Lord. No longer will we worry about having to travel here and there
nor about having the time to do this or that. We shall have all eternity to do whatever we have a mind to do: talk to friends or ride
waves or sit on the porch and sing. No longer will we worry about
wasting time in having fun nor shall we worry that the fun we have
is in some way improper. Never again will we worry about being
in love or losing a love because we shall love our loves in the arms
of the Lord.

This is where my rush to resurrection leads, to peace in the arms
of the Lord. I must try to remember this when my last days come.
Perhaps then I will not be afraid.

The Eve of the Last Week: "Is That All There Is?"

Sometimes when I achieve a goal, I experience a sadness. It almost makes me believe that it is better to be in transit than to arrive. It seems more fun to run the race than to finish. Once done, I look back and wonder, "Is that all there is?"

When I was young, I was haunted by a Peggy Lee song. She was one of my early loves, and her rendition of "Is that all there is?" was a favorite of mine. The song told of a child's growing up through good times and bad, through times of going to the circus, through times of having the house burn down, through times of falling in love. In each case, once the event was over, a melancholy set in. Each happening was greater in expectation than in realization. Once lived through, the event did not seem that extraordinary at all. Each event ended with the refrain: "Is that all there is?"

And so it was (or seemed to be) with my life. For example there was the time that I finally got the courage to send a love letter to my love, Miss Peggy. I even sent her a picture. I was a little boy and she was a mature woman, but I loved her no less intensely. I promised that I would care for her forever (a tough thing to accomplish on an allowance of ten cents a week). I got no response. She must have looked at the picture of scrawny Donald and said, "Is that all there is?"

And I remember all those years of getting educated and finally completing the course and grasping the diploma in my hands and suddenly realizing that now I was supposed to be EDUCATED! I remembered what I did not know and thought, "Is that all there is?"

And I remember all those years of working for big jobs with big responsibilities and big desks, hoping that the bigness of my position would make me big too. I remember the day when I got that big job and walked into my big office and saw written in the dust of my big desk, "Is that all there is?"

I remember my days of wanting to love and to be loved. I said to myself, "If only I can find love, then I will find the ecstasy promised by the love songs drifting from my radio." I found my love and did find ecstasy but found anxiety and worry too. I discovered that love is always fine but that it is only easy when it happens to someone else. I looked at the sunny clouds of my love-filled days and cried, "Is that all there is?"

Every event of my life so far seems to be mixed and incomplete. Every goal achieved seems to create a thirst for more. Every answer poses new questions. And the question is always, "Is that all there is?" Will that same question be asked when I have completed that last great goal of my living, my dying? The day shall come for me, as it did for Jesus, when I shall be on the eve of my last week of this life. Perhaps I shall expect too much of my death as I have often expected too much from life. I seem always to hope for too much. Perhaps it is my woundedness that makes it so. I rush towards perfection on crippled legs. I played my life games as best I could but could not overcome my tiredness. I learned my lessons as best I could but still remained ignorant. I did my jobs as best I could but never felt satisfied with the result. I loved as best I could but could not always do away with loneliness. And thus I fear now that although I will try to die the best I can, the results will not be fulfilling.

On the eve of my last week, I must concentrate on listening for the Lord. I must read again his promises and try to become convinced of them. Reading his words, I can come to see that he does indeed say that I shall be surprised by my death. But I shall be surprised not because I hoped for too much but because I hoped for too little. He promises that I shall not be disappointed with my life beyond death. The message is clear in the words of the revelation made to John:

> I saw new heavens and a new world . . . as beautiful as a lovely
> bride on the day of her wedding. And I heard a voice saying:
> "This is where God lives with men. He will love them and they
> shall be his people and he shall be their God. He shall never leave
> them. And he shall wipe every tear from their eyes, and there shall
> be no more death or mourning, crying out or pain" (see Rev
> 21:1-5).

What the Lord is saying to me is that when I finally reach resurrection, all of my days of unfulfilled hopes will be finished. The Lord himself will give me "all there is," and I shall finally and forever be satisfied.

Sunday of the Last Week: The Ass

Sometimes truly important events can only be conveyed through stories. Such stories may not always be completely true, but they often give insights not taught by bare facts. Our fantasies at very least contain great truths about ourselves. Thus, my story of the Palm Sunday ass may somewhat reflect my own life. Perhaps it expresses the wish of a simple human being to be faithful to an ideal, to make things be "right," to be with someone I love. All of these sentiments are confused and unfocused. Something like the thoughts of a jackass on the great day of his life.

He never got very upset when humans called him an ass. He grew accustomed to the name at an early age. Indeed, his mother always impressed upon him that he was an ass and that he should always act like one. He respected her opinion very much. She should know; she was an ass herself.

Thus he did not find it strange that he should be plodding along a rocky path to the town with this man on his back. To bear other's burdens was his calling in life. It *was* a bit strange that he should be thinking about it, but the events of the day were so odd as to make even an ass stop and think. For example, there was this man on his back. He was a big man, strong from a life lived walking the hills and valleys. And yet the burden of his weight seemed almost nothing. The ass would long remember the caress of his hand.

Then the crowds! The ass had borne many burdens: hay and timber, wheat fresh from the fields, shining silver. Priest and Pharisee had used his services. He had been the ornament of great beauties and the willing playmate of children. But never had he felt the importance of his service as he did now. Never before had he attracted so much attention! The people along the road shouted with joy at seeing him. They cast fragrant palm fronds at his feet so that his every step exploded bursts of sweet fragrance. He thought to himself, "How glad must this man be to be borne by such a great ass!" But the man on his back did not seem to be rejoicing. The ass felt the presence of Sorrow on his back.

That day finished as all days do, but the ass continued to wonder about the Sunday events. He was still thinking about what happened at the end of the week. It was Friday. He had been given the day off because of some feast of the crazy humans he served. His memories of Sunday disturbed him as he stood quietly in his stall; thus he was pleased with the distraction of the crowd noises from outside. He raised his head in excited anticipation. "Perhaps they are coming back to worship me!" he thought. But the crowd rushed by his stall. And they were shouting curses, not cheers.

The man was the object of their fury. He struggled up the narrow street under the weight of a huge piece of wood. His face was a mask of blood. His limbs trembled in agony. The ass could feel the sorrow welling up in his breast. "Why did they not help him? Why did they not take up his burden? Why did they persecute him? Could it be that they did not see who he was? Could they not see, when even an ass could know?" With all the power of his animal lungs he cried, "Do you not see that this is your God?"

For a moment there was a flicker of a smile on the man's face. He had heard over the curses of the crowd the sorrowful bray of an ass.

Monday of the Last Week: "Give Me Five Minutes More"

In the latter days of this life, there sometimes grows a passion to snatch at remembered love and imagined success just one more time. One hurries through daily events believing that the time is running out for a chance to be a great athlete or a great lover or a great thinker. There is the fear that length of years will bring diminished powers. There is a feeling that the "good things of life will soon be over" and thus that one must snatch this day quickly and make the most of it. We rush out to get a little exercise or to find a little love or to do a little philosophy. We rush out like young turkeys to do once again those great things from our cherished past and succeed only in becoming old coots faster. We run and fall on our faces pretending to be something we are not. We become hyperactive as though thereby to deny our fatigue. And we talk a lot. We ask ourselves the Nicodemus question: "How can a man be born again once he is old?" (John 3:4). And then we answer, "By running as fast as he can." We try to buy time by pretending that it is standing still. We pray, "O God, just give me five minutes more before my days are over. Give me a few more days before my rush to resurrection is over."

This is the way that Hezekiah prayed. His story is told by Isaiah (38:1 ff). Hezekiah was mortally ill, and Isaiah was sent to him to deliver the somber message: "Thus says the Lord: Put your house in order for you are about to die. You shall not recover." Hezekiah was despondent. He turned to the wall, prayed his heart out, and wept bitterly. God had pity on him. He sent Isaiah with a reprieve. He told Hezekiah: "I have heard your prayer and seen your tears. I will heal you. In three days I will have you up and about. I will give you fifteen years more." Hezekiah prayed: "Give me five minutes more, only five minutes more" and the Lord gave him fifteen years.

One is tempted to ask "For what purpose?" (One is tempted to ask, that is, if it is not one's own life at stake. We accept personal gifts usually without questioning.) But there is a valid question about life-extension even when one's own life is at issue. If I have lived a long and mottled life, there is no assurance that future years will be any more perfect. Life does not change radically from one year to the next, especially when the years accumulated are quite extensive. Jesus brought Lazarus back to life, but there was not much new in Lazarus' world. Indeed, he ended up somewhat worse off. As soon as he was resurrected, the leaders made plans to kill him (John 12:1-11). As far as we know, Jesus never resurrected a truly old man. Simeon, for example, waited for a long time to see Jesus and then died in peace. He probably would have been much upset if he had been pulled back from his childhood in eternity to experience again the pains of being old in this life. Jesus gave a great gift to his foster father, Joseph, in allowing him to continue his sleep of death. The poor man had earned his rest. Why disturb him with "five minutes more?" Is there ever an advantage in having life continue beyond its appointed time of ending?

Sometimes there do seem to be advantages. If a human being received Hezekiah's gift of fifteen more years, some good things might happen:

in fifteen years you can see children grow and become
  independent;
in fifteen years you can finish a career only recently begun;
in fifteen years you can find your life's great love;
in fifteen years you can become committed to the Lord.

But there is no assurance that an additional fifteen years will be any better than those already experienced. They may be very much worse:

in fifteen years you may see your child die;
in fifteen years you may see your projects fail;
in fifteen years your human loves may leave you;
in fifteen years you may despair.

Once we have set ourselves in life, the future is mostly a reflection of the past. There are no truly "new" vistas; there are no completely "different" places. No matter where we go or how long we live we always carry along the same baggage, namely, ourselves. And it truly would be a miracle if this old bag that is me would change radically in five minutes or even fifteen years. If now I am an elderly curmudgeon, in fifteen years I will likely be an old curmudgeon.

The sobering fact about most human lives is that once we are fixed in our ways, the only truly radical change in our mode of existence comes with death and resurrection. And to prepare for these events, we do not need a great amount of time. There is nothing to pack to be ready for our last steps towards resurrection. There is only something to say. And the words are simple. They are, "Lord, I wish to be with you."

Thus if I have enough time in my last days to mend a few fences here on earth and to make amends with the Lord, then any more time would not help me too much. I am going to go on to resurrection someday. Why not get on with it? Hopefully at the end of my appointed time, my prayer will not be, "Give me five minutes more," but rather the prayer of Monday of Holy Week, "All-powerful God, strengthen and protect me in my weakness."

Tuesday of the Last Week: Bill's Call

We are called to death as well as to life. At the last moment of this life Isaiah's proud boast is true still: "Listen, O distant peoples. The Lord called me from birth, from my mother's womb he gave me my name" (Isa 49:1). There is no such thing as an accidental death in God's eyes. We die when we die, because God has planned it that way. He plans my death as much as he planned that I should live at all or that I should live at this particular time. Thus there is no good time to die nor a bad time to die—there is only *my* time to die. My death will not surprise God, thought it may surprise others. Looking at the event of death, there is a strangeness about it sometimes. God knows when he will call a particular human, but sometimes that call is a surprise to the humans involved. For example there was the call of my friend Bill.

Bill died on Christmas night, much to the surprise of all (including Bill). Bill was an Augustinian priest. On Christmas eve he had said Mass in the home of a young friend who was too sick from cancer to go to church. And Bill said to him: "Don't be scared! Jesus is coming!" Then on Christmas morning Bill said Mass for some old folks who were shut in by the pains of age. They were forced to stay home mostly, biding their time waiting for the new life that awaited them after death. And Bill told them: "Don't be impatient! Jesus is coming!" On Christmas evening Bill dined well with family and friends, sharing memories and speaking about his plans for the New Year with his various classes. Bill, you see, was a teacher. He would teach young people about life, saying to them, "Do good every day! Jesus is coming!" On Christmas night Jesus came, and Bill died.

It was a surprise to us, his friends. We said to each other, "No human should die on the day God is born!" But it happened. Bill died on Christmas night. It seemed as though he and Jesus rushed past each other with a wave as each of them hurried to be born in the other's world. We who were Bill's friends wept at first, but finally we came to realize that there is no day excepted from God's plan for birth and death. Any day is a good day for God to come into our world. Any day is a good day for us to go with God into his world.

Perhaps Bill died on Christmas, because he and Jesus wanted to give that one last sermon to those of us who remained behind and were afraid. The message was simply this: birth and death are not opposed; they are two parts of the same story. Indeed, every day of my lfe this side of death witnesses the continuation of the double process. Every day Jesus rushes to be with me in my life. Every day I rush to be with him on the other side of death.

Bill died on Christmas, but there is nothing strange in that. It just happened to be the day when Jesus called him. And I cannot call it a bad thing. Any day Jesus calls a person home is a fine day. I hope I remember that when my final day comes. As I stand on the last edge of life, I hope I remember Bill's call. Then perhaps I will say to myself: "The Lord called me from birth and he is now calling me to leap through death. He calls me now because it is my time. Now is my time to run and see him."

Wednesday of the Last Week:
"Nothing More Can Be Done"

Sometime during the last week of his life, Jesus must have heard the words that every human being hears (sometimes only deep inside) as death approaches. Someone (perhaps Pilate) said to Jesus: "I am sorry. There is nothing more that can be done."

Perhaps Pilate did not say it in so many words, but he certainly conveyed the message clearly when he washed his hands of Jesus' life and death. The action spoke louder than any words he could choose, just as in our lives the most important messages come to us through action:

knowing that we are loved by being hugged;
knowing that we are alone by being left alone;
knowing that we are coming to the end when they take away our medicines and say to us, "Sleep now, and soon you will feel better" (and they are right).

Thus when Jesus stood before Pilate, he heard Pilate saying to him through the washing: "This day, Jesus, you must leave this life. Nothing more can be done."

For each of us, those words will be said someday. And they will have a double meaning. They will mean what they meant for Jesus, "Soon you will die and nothing can be done to stop it." But they will also mean for us "Nothing more can be done to mess up your life. If you love the Lord now, you will love him forever." Our death will be our triumph.

So too was Jesus' death. At the end he uttered a loud cry that must have frightened his friends. He cried out, "It is finished!" But it was not a cry of despair; it was a cry of triumph. He was telling the world that he was going home and there he would be surrounded by all his loves: that one called Father, that one called Spirit, and maybe (if he does not mess up) even that one who types these words. Jesus was triumphant on the cross of death, because despite his pain he knew that even in his human nature he would live forever. He would carry forever the scars of this life's wounds, but the wounds themselves would no longer hurt. They would be only gentle reminders of what he went through for his friends.

In his last days Jesus suffered terribly. We cannot make light of his wounds and his pain any more than he would make light of ours. His agony was real, just as our agony is real. His human pain was just as real as his human pleasure. His death isolation on Calvary was just as real as his joyous dancing at Cana. But despite the pain Jesus ran forward towards his death. He knew that his death, terrible as it was, would be worth something. There was meaning in his death, and there was love. As he looked down from his cross, he was able to see some who loved him.

His last cry was indeed a cry of triumph. He knew that his suffering would soon be over. He was not sad that he had heard the words "Nothing more can be done" because he knew that nothing more *needed* to be done. His days of loving pain were over. The future would be only days of love.

I hope that I can know that when someone says to me the words. I hope that I rush peacefully to my resurrection when nothing more can be done to hold me back.

Holy Thursday Evening: The Last Gift

As we humans come to the end of life, we feel a special need to leave something of ourselves behind. We may make a will distributing what we own to the people we love or to the causes we care about. We do so because we cannot leave ourselves. We would like to. We would like to never leave our loved ones. But that is impossible. Our rush to resurrection cannot be stopped. We *must* go, but we would like to leave behind some last gift. That is the way Jesus felt too. On the evening before his death, he gathered around him those whom he loved in order to give his last gift. It is good for us to remember the scene.

It was the evening before his death, and Jesus knew it. Judas was even now looking for a good time to betray him. Once the treason was done, his dying would move swiftly. His dying had been orchestrated by the leaders of the people. It was time for Jesus to die. It was thus time for his final farewell gift.

The disciples understood none of this. Few even remembered his earlier prophecy that only through death could life win the day. Few remembered that evening when he had said that he was the way to life, that he was the bread of life. Their great concern at the moment was that the feast of Passover be appropriately observed. They may have sensed the hostility of the religious leaders. They may have hoped that a strict observance of the traditional ritual would save them, would prove that they were friends of the traditional religion, would argue that there was no need to persecute them. In any case as they prepared the meal, they did not realize that they were preparing to eat with the Lord for the last time this side of his death.

Jesus entered the room of banquet and took his place at table. Before he began to eat, he looked at those he loved and said, "One of you will betray me!" The disciples were very upset. These first Christians could not imagine that they could fail. But Jesus knew that they would. He knew that before evening was done they would all run away. He knew that they would deny him in word or action and thus he knew that they needed some final proof that he loved them anyway. They needed a gift to remember him by. Perhaps his gift would not stop them from running away, but it might give them the courage to come back. It might give them the strength to come back again and again after a lifetime of failures and repentance until finally they were confirmed in his love through their death.

And so it was that Jesus on the night before he died took bread, gave a prayer of thanks, and gave it to his friends, saying:

"Take this! This *is* my Body!"

And then he took the cup filled with ordinary wine and gave it to them, saying:

"Take this! This *is* my Blood!"

Then he gave them a final instruction:

"Do this in my memory. Whenever you do this you will remember my life and my death. If you receive me into your life, perhaps you will be better able to face your death."

Rising from the table, Jesus then went out to meet his own death. He left nothing behind but a band of frightened humans, a message to be remembered, and the great sacrament of his Body and Blood.

The Lord had saved his best gift to the very last.

Good Friday: The Day for Dying

In Jesus' rush to Easter the day finally came (as it will to all of us) when he just *had to* die. He had to die, because it hurt too much to stay.

The hurt was partly physical. The pain in trying to keep his poor battered body going must have been immense. As he hung on the cross, he may have thought the same thoughts that we humans think in our last illness: "Why bother struggling against death any longer? Why not just let go?" As Jesus hung on the cross he may have said to himself: "Why try to hold on for an extra hour? I can say all I want to say in three. Why prolong the agony?" As he came closer and closer to the end, Jesus' human spirit became too big for his tattered body. His soul wanted to be *free*, and it bumped against the walls of this life struggling to get through. It wanted *to be through* with this life. His soul simply had to leave his shattered body because it hurt too much to stay. And so shall it be for us someday.

It is not an unusual event—this struggle to be free—in human lives. Even at the very beginning the developing infant must burst free of its wombed confinement if life is to continue. To stay in the dark womb would eventually bring death to both mother and child. We are born from our mother's bodies because the day comes when it simply hurts too much to stay.

As we grow and mature, another time of transition comes. There comes a time when we must leave the protection of family and strike out on our own. We must take responsibility for our lives. If we never grow up, if we never leave the nest, we will never become what we could be. We will suffocate in a narrow life of prolonged childhood. If we are to grow and perfect ourselves, we finally must leave, because it would hurt too much to stay.

Sometimes we must leave a love, because it would hurt too much to stay. Our love may be deep and true, but for some reason it is terribly impractical. Lovers may feel that they cannot live without each other but common sense sometimes dictates that they must. They cannot live out their love without doing terrible injury to each other and perhaps to many others. The love is still deep and true, but oddly enough it is best demonstrated by separation. Sometimes in this life we must leave our loves, because it would hurt too much to stay.

Perhaps this was one of the reasons why Jesus died when he did. He knew that it was only by leaving that he could help his loves. He saved his loves by dying for them. He gave them life by his death. But he helped them in a more ordinary sense too. If he had stayed, his disciples would probably have continued to depend on him for everything. They never would have taken responsibility for their faith. They never would have fought for it. If Jesus had stayed in this life, they would have continued to put all their hopes in this life, hoping that Jesus would take over this world as king and make them his princes and princesses. Perhaps Jesus knew that as long as he remained alive, his disciples would never face up to the reality of their own deaths. They would think more about this life than about any life after death. To help them believe, Jesus needed to die and then come back. He had to help them believe in the reality of human resurrection. He had to leave, because it would have hurt his loves to stay.

Jesus died, but the story does not end there. On Easter morning he rose from the dead. The pressure of his continuing life was too much for his grave to contain. He was alive! Even in his humanity he was gloriously alive! He just had to leave his tomb, because it hurt too much to stay.

So shall it be for us someday. This is his promise.

Holy Saturday: Peaceful Sleep

Death is done; resurrection has not yet come. What shall my condition be at that time of my life? It is hard to imagine. I know that I will be incomplete. My body will quickly disappear, and I will miss it. I agree with St. Augustine that the song, "I ain't got no body!" is more of a lament than a song of joy. My soul will continue. This is the clear message and promise of Christ, but it will be unbodied. What will this unbodied state between death and resurrection be like? St. Augustine suggests that it will be something like being asleep.

If it is like sleep, it will not be too bad at all. In this life sleep is one of the great gifts God gives to embodied spirits exhausted by the toil of everyday living, by mental stress as much as by physical labor. It is no wonder that the disciples slept on the mountain of Transfiguration and in the garden of Gethsemane. On the mountain they were physically tired from their exertion. In the garden they were tired by their crushed hopes and such tiredness is no less real than the tiredness that comes from lifting boxes. By sleep we humans make repairs after the exhaustion of being alive in this world.

Sleep is a blessing on any day, but it is especially so during the days of dying. I am never reluctant to say to dying friends (especially after giving them the Lord in the sacraments), "Sleep now and do not worry about being rude to us." In the last hours the dying seem to move back and forth between time and eternity. They open their eyes to see their loved ones in this life and then close their eyes to

see those waiting for them in the next. In their last sleep perhaps
the Lord himself comes to them saying: "Sleep now. Soon you will
feel just fine."

Once we die, there is no more struggle. Like Jesus on Holy Saturday evening, we rest waiting for the time to get up. It will be a
peaceful waiting but not necessarily unconscious. Perhaps we will
dream. Dreams in this life suggest that it is possible to be at rest
and yet continue having interesting experiences. If we have loved
the Lord (or at least done our best to love the Lord), our dreams
will be only of good things. We will dream of those who loved us
and whom we loved in this life. We will dream of the Lord who
saved us. We will dream of all the fine things waiting for us when
the dawn of resurrection day comes. Though resting, we shall be
watchful. We shall not imagine things. We shall see things as they
really are. We shall see that world that God has promised to us
in his words and works.

We shall be at rest until that great day when the Lord comes
for us. Perhaps the meeting will be like the meeting between Jesus
and Adam. It is described in a very ancient sermon given to the
early Christian community on Holy Saturday:

> The Lord took Adam by the hand and raised him up saying:
> "Awake, O Sleeper, and rise from the dead . . . I order you, O
> Sleeper, to awake . . . Rise up, work of my hands, you who were
> created in my image! Rise, let us leave this place, for you are in
> me and I am in you. Together we form only one person and we
> cannot be separated any more" (Office of Readings: Holy
> Saturday).

Jesus will say something like that to us on the day of our resurrection. We shall wake from our quiet sleep, be united to our mint
fresh bodies, and laugh and run with our loves for eternity.

Easter: Memories

In this life the greatest gift we can give to another human being is the treasure of good memories. In this life only memories last.

We give good memories to each other at every age. The very young give memories of days when life was fresh and sparkling. The very young give us memories of how that first and only day of eternity shall be.

Those in the prime of their lives remind us of how fine it is to be vigorous and full of spunk. They remind us of how it feels to be truly strong and to be doing important things with our lives. Those in the vigor of life remind us of how we shall feel on that first day and only day of eternity.

Those in their last days—those who are very old or very sick— can give us the most precious memory. They can give us a memory of how one can wait patiently for the coming of the Lord. Their last days bravely lived can remind us that the Lord will come for us too on that first and only day of eternity.

Jesus gave us very good memories. Indeed, perhaps that was the main reason why God became a human being. He could have saved us without becoming incarnate. But if he had not lived our human life, he could not have given us such fine memories:

> the memory of a God who understands human happiness and who rejoiced to be able to provide wine for the wedding of a friend;
> the memory of a God who understands human sorrow and who was not ashamed to weep at the grave of a loved one;
> the memory of a God who played with children;
> the memory of a God who went fishing with friends and did not catch anything;
> the memory of a God who forgave a sinner when the humans were getting ready to execute her;
> the memory of a God who understands the human cry, "My God, why have you forsaken me?" because he said the same words himself;
> the memory of a God who so desperately wanted to be with his human friends, that the night before he died he took bread and

wine and gave it to his disciples saying: "This is my Body; this is my Blood. Do this in memory of me."

Jesus gave us all these memories, and then he died. But then he came back from the grave to give us the most precious memory of all, the memory of what living after death might be like:

like Emmaus, walking along a country road in the springtime with dear friends;
like having a picnic on the beach;
like having a loved one ask us, "Do you love me more than the rest?" and being able to answer truthfully, "Yes, I do."

Jesus gave us good memories. But more, he gave us hope. We can hope now because the clear message of his life, death, and resurrection is simply this:

"Jesus Christ, the Son of God, lived our life and conquered our death. And where he is now, we too someday shall be."

Postscript: Balloons

I must admit that I have a "thing" for balloons. They seem such fine symbols of my life. A balloon is a fragile being with only a small opening to the outside world. Its importance comes more from what it contains than what it is. When it is first made, a balloon is not much to look at. It is all wrinkled and scrawny. Left to itself it is not much of anything, but once expanded it becomes a thing of beauty, a colorful delicate ball of nothingness well-suited to delight children and enhance festive occasions. Thus sometimes as I drive along and see a balloon swinging merrily from a mailbox on a country road, I know beyond a shadow of a doubt that there is joy there.

We humans are like balloons in many ways. We begin scrawny and spend most of our adult days trying to expand our lives, filling them with people and careers and things. Sometimes we try to engulf other lives, on the mistaken notion that we become bigger and more important when we consume others. During our days of vigor, we huff and puff to make ourselves larger, desperately afraid of the day when the air will rush out through our cracks, and we will fly away small and insignificant into eternity. We fear the day that we shall literally run out of steam (or, air) and die. That will be that, the end of another punctured balloon.

But the promise that Jesus makes to me and to you is quite different from this depressing scenario. He cannot take away our natural emptiness. That is just the way we are. However he promises that if we let him, he will fill us with himself. Even as we age and seem to be getting smaller and smaller, in fact we will be getting bigger and bigger, if we allow the spirit of the Lord to fill us. He will grow bigger and bigger in us until finally the pressure will become too great and we will die, exploding into the next life forever free of the confined spaces that imprisoned us here. For a while our spirits shall rest, but then at the end of time they will be given back their bodies, bodies that are no longer a pain but filled with glory.

The promise that the Lord makes to me and to you is this: "If you, my love, will only open your life even a little bit to me, I will come and fill you with my own life; whether you are famous or anonymous, whether you are sick or healthy, whether you live a long time or only for a moment, I will continue filling you with my life until your time comes to leap into eternity." Then our troubles will be over. Fragile as we are, we shall never again need to die. Our rush to resurrection will finally be done.